Free Texas

Free things to see and do in the Lone Star State.

By Tab Lloyd

© 2008 Xavier House Publishing. All rights reserved.

ISBN 978-0-9790227-2-2

Printed in the U.S.A.

No part of this book may be reproduced, stored in a retrieval system, or transmitted, in any form or by any means, electronic, mechanical, photocopying, recording, or otherwise, without the prior permission of the author.

The author, staff, and publisher accept no responsibility for loss due to errors, omissions, inaccuracies or inconsistencies incurred within. Readers are encouraged to call ahead, or visit the web-page of any attraction they choose for any information changes.

Final cover design by James Bilodeau, based on the art of Stuart Lloyd.

Contributions to Introduction by James Bilodeau

All photos by Stuart Lloyd

Edited by James Bilodeau

Research assistance by Amanda N. Huffman

For Mike and Connor;
you make the stories meaningful and fun.

Contents

Introduction..13

Churches..23

Buu Mon Buddhist Temple	25
Central Christian Church	27
Central Presbyterian Church	28
Church of the Heavenly Rest, Episcopal	29
First Presbyterian Church	31
Marvin United Methodist Church	32
Saints Cyril and Methodius Catholic Church	34
Saint Francis Church on the Brazos	35
Saint Paul's United Methodist Church	36
Saint Peter the Apostle Catholic Church	38
Saint Stanislaus Polish Catholic Church	40
San Antonio Missions National Historical Park	41
Trinity Episcopal Church	43
Shrine of La Virgen de San Juan del Valle	45

Famous People in Texas.. 47

Babe Didrikson Zaharias Museum	49
Brookshire's World of Wildlife Museum	51
Conrad Hilton Museum	53
Edison Plaza Museum	55
Elisabet Ney Museum in Hyde Park	56

George Paul Museum	58
Haley Memorial Library and History Center	60
John Nance Garner Museum	62
Judge Roy Bean Center	64
Light Crust Doughboys Hall of Fame and Museum	66
Lyndon B. Johnson National Historic Park	68
Mary Kay Museum	70
O. Henry House and Museum	72
Sam Houston Memorial Museum Complex	73
Sid Richardson Museum	75

Trade..77

5 D Custom Hats & Leather	79
Breedlove Dehydrated Foods	81
Bureau of Engraving and Printing	83
The Candle Factory	85
James Leddy Boots	87
Mrs. Baird's Bakery- all places- Fort Worth, San Antonio, Houston, Abilene, Lubbock	89
Nocona Athletic Goods Company	92
Sam Houston Boat Tour	94
Texas Basket Company	95
Wimberley Glass Works, Inc.	96

Art..99

Amon Center Museum	101
Art Center of Corpus Christi	103

Ellen Noël Art Museum of the Permian Basin	104
El Paso Museum of Art	106
First State Bank of Uvalde	108
Kimbell Art Museum	110
Lillie and Hugh Roy Cullen Sculpture Garden	112
Menil Collection	114
The Old Jail Art Center	116
Stark Museum of Art	117

Beer and Wine... 119

Cap*Rock Winery	121
Llano Estacado Winery	122
Piney Woods Country Wines	123
Sister Creek Vineyards	124
Spoetzl Brewery	125
Texas Hills Vineyards	127
Val Verde Winery	128

Farms and Gardens.. 129

Amarillo Zoo in Thompson Park	131
Chihuahuan Desert Gardens at the University of Texas El Paso	132
Houston Arboretum and Nature Center	134
Japanese "Sunken" Tea Garden	136
Sauer-Beckmann Living History Farmstead	137
Mercer Arboretum and Botanic Gardens	138
Sea Center Texas	140

Tyler Municipal Rose Garden 142

Outside.. 143

Alibates National Monument 145
Amistad National Monument 147
Big Thicket National Preserve 149
Cameron Park 151
Cibolo Nature Center 153
Cole Park 155
Lanana Creek Trail 157
Lake Meredith National Recreation Area 159
Rio Bosque Wetlands Park 161

Military.. 163

Fort Bliss 165
Fort Hood 166
Fort Martin Scott 168
Fort Sam Houston- Army Medical Department Museum 170
Texas Military Forces Museum 171
Texas Panhandle War Memorial 173

Historical Places.. 175

1861 Custom Home 177
Carson County Square House Museum Complex 179
Durst-Taylor Historic House and Gardens 181

Gonzales Historical Tours 182
Guenther House 184
Independence Tours 186
La Villita 188
Polly's Chapel 190
Sam Houston Regional Library and Research Center 192
Sterne-Hoya Home 194
The Paramount 196
Tyrrell Historical Library 198
White-Pool House 200

History Museums ... 203

Bell County Museum 205
Border Patrol Museum 207
Central Texas Area Museum 209
Central Texas Oil Patch Museum 210
Deaf Smith County Museum 211
Fire Museum of Texas 213
George Washington Carver Museum
and Cultural Center 215
Hutchinson County Historical Museum 217
Llano County Museum 219
National Ranching Heritage Center 221
Old Jail Museum 223
Old Nacogdoches University Building 225
Smith County Museum 227
Texas Surf Museum 229
Wharton County Museum 230

Wichita Falls Railroad Museum 232

Uniquely Texas 235

The Alamo 237
Capitol Complex 239
Chamizal National Museum 242
Goliad's Historic Downtown Square 244
Gonzalez Memorial Museum 246
Hall of State 248
Luckenbach 250
Odessa Meteor Crater 251
Palo Alto Battlefield National Historic Site ... 253
Rangerette Showcase 254
Washington-on-the-Brazos State Historical Site ... 255
XIT Museum 257

Appendix 259

INTRODUCTION

Introduction

Even in this day and age of super corporations, world trade, stock market gambles, and a general preoccupation for wealth – many things are still free. Tourism today is a multi-billion dollar industry which is growing at a rapid pace. Mega-amusement parks, roadside attractions, and family adventures pop up across the countryside on a daily basis. Many states are latching onto the tourism industry in attempt to bring in additional revenue to tight state budgets. States such as: New Mexico, Maryland, Kentucky, and Texas have been at the fore-front of this movement. With aggressive advertising, trade show promotion, and tax incentives, tourism has grown tremendously within these states. Most of the increase in the number of attractions are for-profit ventures, but even in the booming for profit tourism industry; there are many opportunities for free entertainment.

Reasons things are free

With all of the for-profit tourism ventures popping up, it may seem odd that there are places that still do not charge an admission fee. There are many reasons for this, and they are as varied as the attractions themselves. The one common theme, that all the free attractions have, is they all have a specific goal other than profit. Some things are free simply based on the mission of the attraction.

Churches are an example of this. Churches have the specific purpose of sharing their faith and traditions. Churches, especially Catholic churches, are commonly open most of the day and night for silent reflection and prayer. The churches in this book are known for the beauty of their design and decor and gladly welcome visitors who want to admire their beauty.

Zoos and gardens serve the purpose of preserving different species of animals and plants. Gardens and arboretums are commonly run by clubs whose members provide the labor for the upkeep of the flora. Many of these gardens serve as educational facilities and test gardens for new plant species and growing techniques.

Museums, both art and history, have a long tradition of being free to visitors. Recently a number of museums have started charging admission fees, although most just a few dollars. The majority of museums are still free, and this will probably remain the case for many years since most museums are run by universities and historical societies. These organizations have an interest in educating visitors about the history of their area, as well as building respect for the subject matter of the museum.

Government entities are well known for offering free attractions. Just as most attractions are free in Washington D.C., the same thing is true in the states. One purpose for governments offering free museums and activities is to allow the public to "see their tax dollars at work." Museums on military bases often serve as military recruitment tools. State capitol building tours foster pride and confidence the state government system. Fish hatchery tours show the government making effective use of tax dollars for the good of nature. Anytime politicians are involved there is an extensive effort to build good public relations with potential voters!

Much like the government, businesses also like to build good public relations. Unlike the government, businesses are trying to make a profit. Even with this motivation, businesses have seen the need in providing free recreational opportunities to their current and future customers. The trade tour, in which visitors get to see first hand the production of a product, has been an emerging attraction. Businesses find if they allow people to see their product being made it builds consumer confidence in the product itself. It is common for people to feel more connected to a product and become loyal repeat customers. Businesses take these tours very seriously and make sure that their tours are high quality, entertaining experiences. The trade tour also gives the visitor the impression that the company is "giving something back" to the community. Recently some businesses have started charging visitors for their tours. Many people think that this is a bad business practice, because it negates some of the positive public relations benefits of the tours.

How Free Things Stay in Business

One of the oldest business mantras is "Don't give away the store"! How can something stay in business if their sole purpose is not to charge for their service? Businesses that offer free trade tours obviously make a profit from the sale of their products, but what about the attractions with nothing to sell? The answer to this question is their ability to operate on a shoestring budget and creatively raise funds.

Grants

One major revenue stream for free attractions comes in the form of grants. Grants are blocks of money that are awarded to an entity based on its need, and the service that it provides to the public. Although most grants come from government entities, there are also a number of grants that are awarded by major corporations. Winning grants is not an easy task. An attraction wishing to apply for a grant must fill out the appropriate applications, and must be able to convince the issuer of the grant of their worthiness to receive the grant. The competition for grants is very competitive so attractions end up getting very few of the awards that they apply for.

Although almost all free attractions depend on grant money to make ends meet, some do have the luxury of having a regular budget. Some attractions, mostly of a historical nature, are actually provided a portion of their operating budget from local city and county governments. To get this type of funding the organization's purpose is usually to display artifacts and information about the history of the local town or county. Government attractions will usually be mostly funded through a regular annual budget. Whether the organization is partially funded, or completely funded through government dollars, the amount of funding given is almost always based on the number of people the attraction serves. Most of the time an attraction will use a guest book to keep track of the number they serve. If you see a guest book please fill it out. If you don't your favorite attraction may lose important funding.

Memberships

One innovative way free attractions have found to increase funding is through the sale of memberships. History museums have done this for some time by offering memberships to a historical society that oversees the museum's operation. Although selling memberships is not a common practice among businesses offering trade tours – the sale of memberships is becoming a regular occurrence. For their membership fee the member usually is entitled to receive a newsletter and gets invited to various private functions and social gatherings. The members usually consist of high profile community and business leaders, or people who want to be. Memberships are often bought for the status and networking opportunities among business people. Since membership sales have been such an effective money generating tool, some "for-profit" organizations have also started membership programs.

Donation Box

In addition to innovative membership programs, free attractions also rely on the most basic methods of fund raising. The most basic form of fundraising is the traditional donation box. Nowadays the donation box occupies a prominent place near the attraction's entrance and is often decorated to be easily noticed. The humble donation box still is one of the most effective means of fundraising, as well as the least intrusive. Sometimes an attendant will make a request for a donation, but this is a very rare occurrence.

Gift Shops

The traditional gift shop has been a stalwart in the fundraising process. Many gift shops today are stocked with high quality items that pertain to the attraction itself. Gone are the days of the tacky t-shirt and plastic cups. The increasing popularity of the internet has led to the creation of online gift shops which offer the same high quality souvenirs as the gift shop on location. The concept of the gift shop remains the same; profits generated are used for the attraction's upkeep.

Volunteers

For a free attraction to stay open more than money is needed, a motivated workforce is essential. This motivated workforce almost always works for free. In almost all cases an attraction will have just one or two employees that draw a salary of any kind. If an employee draws a salary it is usually one that is lower then they could normally get with their level of education and experience. The highest level staff person at an attraction can commonly be found filling out grant applications, seeking donations, sweeping the floor, giving tours, and cleaning bathrooms. Most of these staffers do their job for the love of what they do. Most of the additional workers are unpaid volunteers.

Donations

In this book, free means free. Every effort has been made to weed out the "free" attractions from the ones with a specific "suggested donation." If you wish to donate to any attraction you see, great! Donate in the amount you feel is fair based on your enjoyment. If you choose to buy souvenirs on your trip, please consider shopping at a free attraction's gift shop. If you feel like donating, and don't see a donation box, just ask any staffer and they will be more then happy to accept your gift.

The Cost of Entertainment

There is no doubt that things are not as affordable as they used to be. The hard earned dollar simply doesn't go as far. In addition to ever rising fuel costs, admission fees to pretty much every type of event or attraction has shot up in recent years. It is typical for a museum or aquarium to charge $9.00 or $10.00 per person. With the typical family of five that would be $45-50 just to get in the door. If the family wants to go to an amusement park, the gate entrance can cost as much as $20 to $25 per person. This would mean a family of five will spend over $100 for a day of fun, not including food, gas, and parking!

Why *Free Texas*?

When I was growing up, my family was not wealthy by any means. In fact, by most standards we lived in poverty. We did not have money to travel anywhere but the occasional trip to relatives' houses. However, my mother provided many experiences for me through trips to the library. We may not have done much, but read we did. Through those books, I was able to travel around this world and a number of others as well. Fascinating stories of even the simplest things filled my mind and enabled me to see connections across cultures and time. For this, I am thankful.

Now that I am grown, I work to instill this love of stories in my own children. Summer is our favorite time of the year, because it takes us many places through the doors of the library. But one thing my husband and I can provide for our boys that my family was not able to provide for me, is experience. So, while exploring new lands through books, we also explore the old land in which we live through travel. There's nothing like going to the Gonzales Jail Museum to hear the 1921 story of the "innocent" convict, Albert Howard. Swearing his innocence, Howard cursed the town's clocks to never work again after his execution; they haven't worked since. My boys ask of his innocence, cringing at the thought of being housed in such a horrible place for something someone else did.

Stories are everywhere—and in everything. While some folks have put a price on their stories, chances are, good stories do not cost much. And the best ones? They are freely given. When I asked Cile Ambrose why she offered her museum, the Central Texas Museum in Salado, free to the public, she answered quite plainly, as if I should already have known. "Because Texas IS free. We're a free state, we have a free spirit, we are a free country, we're a free people, and when we have a good thing, we want to share it with everyone. How can you put a price tag on that?" It's true- when you have a good thing, chances are, you just want to share- share the story, the excitement, the opportunity for knowledge. So this book is full of people like Cile, who want to share their lives, stories and history with others, just because.

Now, very few places in this book can one go for entertainment. Entertainment is a service, and from elementary economics lessons, we know that services are given in exchange for something—usually money. Rather, the attractions in this book are more learning opportunities—to experience our past as a state—a nation—a people. What about the out-of-state visitors? We welcome ya'll, too. We will share our stories with anyone who will take the time. But, you have to give it freely. Some places you will like, others may not be your cup of Texas Tea. It's up to you to decide, and there's no other way to do that than to get out and explore our Free Texas.

CHURCHES

Buu Mon Buddhist Temple

2701 Proctor St.

Port Arthur, TX 77640

(409) 982-9319 or 9199

www.buumon.org

Buu Mon Buddhist Temple was established in 1980 in Beaumont, Texas. The temple then moved to Orange, and finally settled in Port Arthur in 1986 into a former Baptist/Catholic Church building. Renovation under Abbot Thich Huyen Viet replaced the steeple of the building with an upturned stupa (monastery building) and brought in a seven-foot bronze Buddha to rest on the front alter. In 1988, Venerable Huyen Viet began the lotus and lily gardens. They quickly became the "jewel of Buu Mon Temple."

The lotus (type of water lily) is Buddhism's most significant symbol, representing enlightenment and purity of mind. The flower, like man, grows from the mud and earth, and then emerges, growing and reaching for the sky towards enlightenment. The monks of Buu Mon take great care in tending the lotus and lily gardens. Day-blooming and night-blooming lilies sparkle in hues from deep magenta-red to clarity-white, while lotus blossoms reach 4 to 8 feet over the water surface, gilded in nothing but the rich colored petals.

Practicing Buddha's message of nonviolence and universal tolerance, monks at Buu Mon welcome people of all religions as visitors to the temple and Water Gardens. They are happy to provide historical and informational tour lectures and answer any questions visitors may have about any aspect of the temple or the four gardens. Weekly classes on Vipassana (insight) meditation are offered Wednesday evenings and the temple has a Chanting Service on Sunday afternoons. Buu Mon hosts a number of annual celebrations, including the Lotus Garden Festival, Southeast Texas Bamboo Festival, Lunar New Year, and the Lantern Festival (other religious celebrations are connected with the festivals as well). Visitors are welcome to come during the festivals, as well as other times during the year. The monks are happy and willing to spend time with visitors, but as a courtesy, they ask visitors to call and make arrangements prior to coming.

TEXAS FUN FACT:

The name Texas comes from Tejas, an Indian word meaning friendly.

Central Christian Church

2611 Wesley

Greenville, TX 75403

(903) 455-1373

www.cccgreenville.com/history2.htm

Designed by James E. Flanders, a Chicago-style architect, the 1899 Central Christian Church building is a towering jewel in the town of Greenville. Located in the outskirts of Dallas, Greenville boasts this Gothic revival structure as housing one of the oldest continually meeting church groups in the area.

Early beginnings of the congregation date back to as early as 1848 as members met in farm houses. After a revival in 1852, members gathered more formally, and in 1879 a wooden meeting house was erected. As the congregation grew, they were in need of a larger building. Construction of Flanders' design started in 1898. 1899 brought the $23,000 completion and dedication of the church's new home.

Mrs. Virginia King is credited as a great contributor for the newly chartered Central Christian Church, donating nearly half the cost of the grounds, building, furnishings, the first organ, and the west art glass window, which is dedicated to her mother, Mrs. Ann M. Chandler. The King Memorial Prayer Chapel is named for Mrs. King.

Although the Central Christian Church building underwent remodeling in 1948 and a $250,000 renovation in 1986, the old charm remains steadfast. Cables and pulleys from a former removable wall are still visible, and the Chicago art glass includes faceted jewels and mouth-blown glass from Germany. The pipe organ hosts 819 pipes from ½ inch to 17 feet.

Central Presbyterian Church

309 South Church St.

Paris, TX 75460

(903) 784-4381

www.parispresbyterian.com

After Texas declared herself an independent nation, many of America's religious leaders saw the opportunity to spread their faith. Foreign missions were established in the Republic of Texas, and this is where Central Presbyterian Church in Paris finds its beginnings. CPC was established as a Cumberland Presbyterian Church in 1844, maintained by circuit-rider Rev. Sam Corley. A string of brick and frame churches were built through the years, up until 1916. Despite the church family's efforts, a fire tragically took the building preceding the current one. The congregation had abandoned the name "Cumberland" in 1908, but refused to give up on the church after the fire took their home. In 1917, Central Presbyterian Church opened the doors of their new red brick home for worship.

Visitors today can find strength and tenacity in CPC's story. The oldest church in Lamar County stands strong in the 1917 building. Inside, tourists will find a taste of the old world in the amber-hued stained glass windows—some are decorative, while others tell stories of Jesus. In addition to the beauty of the building, the congregation is known for its musical performances and worship, accompanied by the immensely proportioned pipe organ.

Though the building itself is not large, the history as an American Mission to the Republic of Texas is worth the trip. While in Paris, visitors can also see "Jesus in Cowboy Boots" in the Evergreen Cemetery amongst many other carved memorials (corner of Church and Evergreen Streets). The "Texanized" miniature 65-foot Eiffel Tower, complete with cowboy hat, is also a popular Texan roadside photo opportunity (corner of Jefferson and Collegiate).

Church of the Heavenly Rest, Episcopal

602 Meander

Abilene, TX 79602-1099

(325) 677-2091

www.chrabilene.com

Shortly after Abilene's establishment as a town in 1881, Episcopal parishioners granted the citizens a new mission in the area. Saint Paul's Mission was instantly popular, growing with the town. In 1883 the congregation built the "Little Stone Church", with most of the money donated by Col. Josiah Stoddard Johnson, a well-established Abilene businessman. In 1885, the renamed Church of the Heavenly Rest achieved parish status. Within the next 35 years, the church had a number of rectors; many did not stay but a few years.

In 1920, Reverend Willis Gerhart, a.k.a. "Parson" came to Heavenly Rest. A better man was not known in the Texas Plains. Parson led his church by example, often welcoming the integration of differing faiths. Stories about Parson's giving nature still circulate the congregation, and it has been said that his reputation as a reverent, fair man made believers from just about anyone. The "Little Stone Church" flourished, but the building was torn down and property sold in order to purchase a larger plot of land for a new, more spacious sanctuary. The old stones were incorporated into the new building, completed in 1956. Parson retired in 1957.

The current building for the Church of the Heavenly Rest is astonishing. The Leuters limestone bricks create a luminescent aura against the sky, true to its name. Inside, carved wood adorns the baptismal font, and stained glass radiates throughout the rounded, peaked windows—a pattern held in doorways as well. True to the Gothic Revival style, the church was built from the ground up, with no steel reinforced frame. Symbolic items are inlayed within various structures in the building. A stone from King Solomon's mine, pebbles from Mount Sinai, a stone from Canterbury, a brick from the first church in Jamestown, Virginia, and of course, the building material and furniture from the original

"Little Stone Church." Although the Gothic style is popular for Texas churches of this era, the building feels old and new all at once, as the church carries its members from the past into the future.

Church office hours are Monday through Friday, 9:00 a.m. to 12:00 p.m. and 1:00 p.m. to 4:00 p.m. Visitors are welcome (and enjoyed) during these hours, but calling ahead will ensure that the tour guide is available. The church asks that only the outside of the building is photographed.

TEXAS FUN FACT:

More wool comes from the state of Texas than any other state in the United States.

First Presbyterian Church of Georgetown

703 Church Street

Georgetown, TX 78626

(512) 863-2281

www.fpcgeorgetown.org

First Presbyterian's sanctuary, constructed in 1873, is the oldest in Georgetown. The founding members began meeting and worshipping in nearby Round Rock in 1854, and by 1855, they moved to Georgetown. The former building hosted the town's first public school from 1867-1873 when the present building was completed. Shortly before its completion, the Presbyterian Church experienced a split due to Civil War and Union fidelity differences. Northern and Southern congregations remained segregated until the 1890's when the northern church disbanded and sold the building to its southern half.

The First Presbyterian Church bought their bell in 1877; it has rung every Sunday since its purchase. In 1895, the building was remodeled into the present Gothic styling, and a belfry and steeple were added in 1913. Through many years of growth and renovation, the church facility is now expanded, including classrooms, a fellowship hall, administration offices, and much more. Visitors to Georgetown will find the simple construction and minimal decoration typical of southern Protestant religious groups. Basic crosses are the extent of much of the décor, reminiscent of the down-to-earth approach to worship. The building is accessible only during office hours or worship services: Monday through Friday 8:30 a.m. to noon and 1:00 p.m. to 4:30 p.m. and 8:00 a.m. until 12:30 p.m. on Sundays.

First Presbyterian Church is recognized as a State of Texas historic Site. Georgetown is also home to other recognized church buildings. See www.georgetown-texas.org/churches.htm for pictures and historical details.

Marvin United Methodist Church

300 W. Erwin Street

Tyler, TX 75702

(903) 592-7396

www.marvinumc.com

Marvin United Methodist Church originated in the Tyler area as the Methodist Episcopal Church—South, first meeting in homes, and later in Adams Blacksmith Shop. In 1848, the congregation purchased land, and by 1852, a two-story building was complete. The church shared the structure with the local Masonic Lodge, and during the Civil War, it served as a hospital, as so many churches did.

By 1888, the members decided to build a new structure rather than repair the worn and damaged original. Construction was complete in 1891, and the church was renamed Marvin United Methodist, after Confederate States of America Chaplain Bishop Enoch Mather Marvin. His powerful ministries and sermons were known throughout the area during the struggles of the Civil War. The next one hundred years brought growth and much construction for the Tyler church. The building now has classrooms, office space, a chapel, and a third floor dedicated to youth ministries.

Throughout the growth, the grandness of Marvin United Methodist remains. The Gothic Revival red brick structure is trimmed with limestone, and cloistered walkways open to an exquisite inside courtyard with a fountain. Inside, stained and leaded hand-blown glass enrich the sanctuary with jewel-colored shapes and symbols. Depictions of a few Bible stories line the back wall of the sanctuary and are the only human images seen (besides the members, of course!). Both the sanctuary and chapel have carved wood decorative panels—elegant yet simple—as their focal points, and appropriately sized pipe organs. The cross-topped steeples stand tall, as Marvin United Methodist remains a literal pillar in the Tyler community for over 150 years.

The Marvin United Methodist Church office is open 8:30 a.m. to 4:30 p.m., Monday through Friday. If visitors cannot make it to Tyler on a Sunday, the weekday office hours are the best times to visit. However, select Sundays have a visiting advantage; in addition to joining this great group of people for worship service, a guided tour of the building and its history is provided afterwards. Call ahead if planning to be in town, to make sure the tour is on the day's schedule. Either way, this piece of history is well worth the trip.

TEXAS FUN FACT:

MUMC also sponsors Boy Scout Troop 363.

Saints Cyril and Methodius Catholic Church

306 South Avenue F

Shiner, TX 77984

(361) 594-3836

www.shinercatholicchurch.org

With Shiner's deep German and Czech roots, it is not surprising to find Saints Cyril and Methodius Catholic Church, named for the saints who first brought Christianity to Bohemia and Moravia. Amazingly beautiful, the present structure replaced the original 1891 building in 1921 by E. Wahrenberger's red brick Romanesque Revival Style design—complete with cut stone detailing on the pinnacles and buttresses. The 112 foot high steeple towers above anything else in the small town of Shiner, across from the railroad tracks that brought original settlers to the area.

Inside, religious icon statues populate the perimeter, bringing the old-world to life. The six floor-to-ceiling "late stained" glass windows, imported from Bavaria, depict not only religious events, but the inscriptions share memories and sentiments from the early members. An elaborate white and gold alter sits below a domed mural of Christ in the Garden of Gethsemane. Angels guard over the congregation in a mural above the altar's archway, while hand carved wooden crosses guard the 3-dimensional Stations of the Cross.

Outside, visitors can see meditation and prayer grottos, the Shiner Catholic School campus, and the Shiner Catholic Cemetery while enjoying the structure and detail of Saints Cyril and Methodius Catholic Church. Texas historical markers site the importance of both the Church and the school (formerly known as Saint Ludmila's Academy) in Shiner's history.

Saint Francis Church on the Brazos

315 Jefferson Ave

Waco, TX 76701

(254) 752-8434

http://www.austindiocese.org

Saint Francis began in 1924 as a mission. Franciscan missionaries came from Spain and raised the wooden building to meet the increasing need of Mexican citizens in the Waco area. Miss Fannie G. Smith donated the land and house next to the mission and is still used today as the house of the Priests. The original church burned in 1928, and by 1931, the current building was complete—a mirror replica of Mission San Jose in San Antonio.

In 1957, Saint Frances Church was the site of the first Cursillo de Cristiandad in the United States—an active renewal movement of the Catholic Church that begins with a three day course—a *cursillo*—to help members develop spirituality in the secular world. Saint Frances Church is known as the cornerstone of this movement, made possible by the works of Fr. Gabriel Fernandez.

Within the church's colorfully tiled interior walls, life-sized paintings of the Stations of the Cross (by Spaniard Pedro Juan Barceló) lead the way to a large domed fresco portraying Saint Francis' vision of God and early struggles of Franciscan monks. Intricate gold and white moulding frames the painted designs as well as the various shrines throughout the church interior.

Saint Francis Church is one block southwest of the Brazos River. On the banks, visitors can see Waco's 1870 Historic Suspension Bridge. The north side of the bridge is home to two of Waco's city parks. Tree lined Indian Spring is on the west with a Riverwalk trail. MLK, Jr. Park, on the east, has an overlook tower that is the perfect spot for photographers looking for the "great shot" of Downtown Waco.

Saint Paul's United Methodist Church

5501 South Main

Houston, TX 77004-6917

(713) 528-0527

www.stpaulshouston.org

St. Paul's United Methodist Church began as a congregation in 1905 with land given by Mrs. J.O. Ross on the corner of Milam and McGowen in downtown Houston. The original building, a Byzantine-style Grecian domed structure, opened in 1909. After significant member growth, the congregation sold the building to Second Baptist Church in 1927, and began construction on their new home on property purchased from the Hermann estate. The Church on Main and Calumet was designed by Alfred C. Finn—designer of many well-known city structures, including the San Jacinto Monument, the Houston Coliseum and Music Hall.

St. Paul's was completed in 1930; the modified English Gothic construction includes a number of design and décor symbols. The ceiling, similar to the hull of a ship, remembers early seafaring Christians who worshipped under their overturned ships. "Antique stained" glass windows share the story of Christ and the early beginnings of the Methodist Church. Crosses, candles, grapes, roses, angels, and other symbols are present in ornate carvings, paintings, or actual items. The intricately designed front Great Organ (The Madison and Martha Farnsworth Organ) stretches from floor to ceiling, with 84 ranks and 4,569 pipes ranging from 32 feet to the size of a pencil. The matching Gallery Organ in the balcony hosts 12 ranks and 732 pipes—smaller, yet impressive as well. Lucky visitors may enjoy the treat of walking into an organist's practice session. Informational pamphlets about the sanctuary and its symbols, as well as the history of the Church, are available inside the building.

St. Paul's United Methodist Church is open daily for visitors; however, St. Paul's hosts many weddings and ceremonies. Visitors should use the Fannin Street entrance to view the building (other doors are locked during non-scheduled events). Guided tours can be arranged for groups or individuals by calling the Church office. Check the website or call for worship times.

TEXAS FUN FACT:

The first word spoken from the moon on July 20, 1969, by astronaut Neil Armstrong, was "Houston". Armstrong earned the rank of Eagle Scout while in the Boy Scouts of America. Two-thirds of all pilots and scientists serving as astronauts since 1959 have had scouting experience.

Saint Peter the Apostle Catholic Church

202 W. Kronkosky St.

Boerne, TX 78006

(830) 816-2233

www.stpetersboerne.com

In the early 1860's, deacon Emil Fleury came to Boerne with the mission, from Bishop Claude Dubuis of the Galveston Archdiocese, to build the town's first Catholic church. Eager and willing, Fleury hired men from Fredericksburg, and worked alongside them to construct the hilltop limestone building on the south side of Cibolo Creek. Many of the community members helped out as well, including George W. Kendall (said to have helped to honor his Catholic wife). One story shares a time when the deacon was so tired from his daily work that instead of going to bed, he fell asleep on the scaffolding. Indians attacked that night, and Fleury woke the next day to find his horse dead and his bed shot full of arrows, truly blessed for dedicating himself to the construction of the church building. By 1866, the church was complete, presented to the Archdiocese debt-free, as Fleury had most materials and labor donated.

In 1920, the membership outgrew the little church, and another structure was built in the style of San Antonio's Mission Concepción. Fleury, in his seventies, laid the cornerstone for the new building once again created from native limestone; it was complete in 1923. By the 1990's, the congregation had once again outgrown the structure, and after a dispute over the historical significance of the 1923 church, the church compromised and encompassed the former building as part of the new rather than their original plans to demolish and start anew.

Today's Saint Peter the Apostle Catholic Church is spacious and airy— the sanctuary can now seat 800 comfortably. While the main sanctuary is not lined with stained glass, typically found in Catholic church buildings, the clear windows allow members and visitors to enjoy the outside beauty of the Texas Hill Country. The 1923 area retains the rectangular stained glass and the more customary feel. The combination of styles work together to blend time-honored traditions with a fresh, contemporary vision; combined, they retain a respectful, religious feeling that is ageless.

TEXAS FUN FACT:

The city of Boerne was made famous by the landmark case City of *Boerne v. Flores* which made it all the way to the U.S. Supreme Court.

TEXAS FUN FACT:

George W. Kendall is known as the "Father of Sheep Business in Texas." He promoted Texas Hill Country as prime sheep range, regularly writing about it in his New Orleans-based paper, the Picayune. He was the first to use vats to dip his flock for disease prevention.

Saint Stanislaus Polish Catholic Church

602 Seventh Street

Bandera, TX 78003

(830) 460-4712

www.ststanislaus.us

Saint Stanislaus Polish Catholic Church boasts itself as the "Second oldest Polish Parish in the United States," and is younger than the church in Panna Maria, Texas by a mere six weeks. In 1855, sixteen immigrant families settled in Bandera, and soon erected their first church building—a 20'X30' log structure. 1874 brought the construction of the limestone convent to provide housing for the nuns who taught and served at the school. The current church building was built in 1876, also from native limestone. Small changes were made throughout the years, including gothic lighting and a complete interior makeover to celebrate its centennial in 1976. The membership recently came together for another refurbishing, and today the building looks as young as ever.

Inside, the pastel frescos include angelic forms and accounts of St. Stanislaus' story. On the church grounds, visitors can see the original convent, now a museum commemorating the lives of the original Polish settlers and their descendants. A Texas State Historical Marker pays respect to the grounds as well. Beside the museum is a meditation garden, leading to the St. Stanislaus Cemetery. The garden sits under an incredible live oak tree, encircled with elegant Station of the Cross monuments.

The church is open at various times of the day for mass and ministries, and touring the grounds is always welcome. The museum has posted hours, but guests are advised to call the church office if planning a visit to ensure that the museum is staffed.

San Antonio Missions National Historical Park

2202 Roosevelt Ave.

San Antonio, TX 78210

(210) 932-1001

www.nps.gov/saan

Spanish missions were not churches alone, but rather communities created by the Spaniards to convert the native Coahuiltecan Indians to Catholicism. While the church served as the center of the community, missions also included housing, schools, farms and other vocational activities (such as pottery or basket weaving)—all of which fostered a self-sufficient society for the members. The National Historical Park in San Antonio encompasses four links to these past communities: Mission Concepción, Mission San José, Mission San Juan, and Mission Espada. The missions are tied together by a 15 mile network of *acequias*, gravity flow ditch systems, which irrigated the land, making farming possible and productive. Each of the mission churches still hold mass and the grounds are used as eloquent backdrops for weddings and other festivities.

Mission Concepción is the first stop on the San Antonio Mission Trail. Originally established in East Texas, Concepción relocated to San Antonio in 1731 with Missions San Juan and Espada. The church's twin towers watch over the tree covered grounds, and a small side garden pays homage to St. Francis and St. Mary. Once covered with colorful frescos, traces of the early Christian and Native American art can still be seen inside the building.

The next stop is San José, the largest of the missions. Visitors can view a 20 minute film, "Gente de Razón" (People of Reason), about the missions' beginnings, told through the eyes of the native Coahuiltecan Indians. Touring the enclosed grounds of San José can easily take hours to enjoy, exploring the way of life for the mission's occupants in the 1700's. The Church is central to the community; the outside façade is speckled with stone carvings of angels and saints. Past the church, visitors can learn about the *acequias* and see a reconstructed water-powered grain mill.

Mission San Juan, originated in East Texas, moved to the banks of the San Antonio River in 1731. The three bells on top of the Church are found charming by tourists, but the awe comes from the wooden cross in the middle of the complex, surrounded by prickly pear cactus.

The last mission on the trail is Mission Espada. The oldest of the East Texas missions moved in 1731, Espada was founded in 1690 as San Francisco de los Tejas. Vocational training was the focus of this mission, still apparent through the bricks and glass work completed by the mission artisans. Mission Espada has the best preserved examples of *acequias*, and the Espada Aqueduct is visible on the drive between Missions San Juan and Espada. The Espada Aqueduct is the oldest Spanish water channel in the U.S., and is still used by farmers today.

The San Antonio Missions National Park is a trip that can be taken in parts or as a whole—as time permits (from an hour to all day). Road maps are available for drivers or bikers at any of the mission visitor centers. The National Parks Service also provides online curriculum and lesson guides, as well as "Junior Ranger" activity programs for children visiting the mission sites. The visitor centers and missions are open daily, 9:00 a.m. to 5:00 p.m., except Thanksgiving, Christmas Day and New Year's Day. Guided tours are available; see website or call for specific times.

TEXAS FUN FACT:

Most National Parks have a "Junior Ranger" program in which children are able to complete activities and workbooks about the park to earn a certificate and "Junior Ranger" badge. The badges and certificates are park specific.

Trinity Episcopal Church
2216 Ball St.

Galveston, TX 77550

(409) 765-6317

www.trinitygalv.org

Trinity Episcopal Church is one of the two oldest churches in Galveston, founded in 1841 by Reverend Benjamin Eaton. The towering Gothic building was completed in 1857, and includes decorative columns inside the sanctuary added after the completion. The columns provide no structural support, but somehow their presence reassured the early members of the potential strength and endurance of the new building. Through the years, the 1857 structure has survived a number of storms, fires, floods, and a yellow fever epidemic, sustaining major damage only when the 1900 storm destroyed the south wall. The church was closed for two years during the Civil War. The pews were used as hospital beds during the Great Battle of Galveston; the building itself was hit by a cannon ball during the battle. The hole is still visible today.

In 1844, Rev. Eaton started the Trinity Episcopal School for boys, but the yellow fever epidemic and lack of appropriately skilled teachers forced the school to close. It reopened in 1873, this time offering services to both boys and girls, and closed again shortly after for unknown reasons. 1952 brought schooling back to the church, starting with Pre-K to 1st grades. The Trinity Episcopal School now provides education for students through the eighth grade.

Reverend Eaton passed away on Palm Sunday, 1871, while giving a sermon. During his talk, he announced that the Angel of Death had come for him, and collapsed, dead. He remains at Trinity—his body is buried in a crypt under the alter, while his spirit of dedication lives on through the welcoming members of the congregation.

Members of the Trinity Episcopal Church are most proud of their large stained glass windows, and rightfully so. Twenty windows depicting various religious events and symbols adorn the sanctuary, including two windows by Tiffany Studios in New York. The Tiffany windows feature the famous opalescent glass that changes colors during the day, based on outside variances. The 1904 window is especially significant in that it is signed by Louis Comfort Tiffany, and is the largest and oldest one of its kind that has remained intact throughout all natural disasters.

Another point of interest is the church's 69-rank Austin pipe organ, hosting 4,086 pipes. The organ, as well as bell chimes, is played regularly during worship services and other special community events. Trinity has regularly scheduled prayer and worship services, contact the website or call for details.

TEXAS FUN FACT:

In 1926, Trinity Episcopal Church was raised 4 ½ feet as a preventative measure for flood damage. It was raised by hand operated jacks to the beat of a drum.

TEXAS FUN FACT:

TEC sponsors Boy Scout Troop 104.

Shrine of La Virgen de San Juan del Valle

400 N. Virgen de San Juan Blvd.

San Juan, TX 78589

(956) 787-0033

www.olsjbasilica.org

Early Spanish missionaries in Jalisco, Mexico placed a statue of the Immaculate Conception in San Juan de Los Lagos, knowing the traditional and special devotion Spanish Catholics have with the Virgin Mary. On this site in 1623, a young girl was brought back to life in San Juan de Los Lagos through prayers to Saint Mary in the presence of this statue. The image was then known as La Virgen de San Juan de Los Lagos.

The migration of Mexicans into Texas brought the love and devotion for Saint Mary, with special attention to the image from their homeland in San Juan de Los Lagos. In 1949, Father Jose' Maria Azpiazu brought in a replica of the Jalisco statue to the church in San Juan, Texas. The numbers of visitors increased enormously, so much that the parish built a shrine dedicated on May 2, 1954.

On October 23, 1970, Francis B. Alexander crashed a small rented plane into the Virgen de San Juan del Valle Shrine. Although the building was occupied and eventually destroyed by fire, Alexander was the only death that day. The image of la Virgen was recovered completely unharmed.

In 1980, a new shrine was built. The property was dedicated as a National Shrine in 1998, and in 1999 it was designated as a Basilica. The immense building can now seat 1,800, and houses the statue of la Virgen as the main focal point. Stained glass adds to the Hispanic feel, with rounded concentric rectangular shapes and the use of reds, oranges and blues. Mission style bells are on the grounds as are the Stations of the Cross—life sized statues portray this journey of Jesus over ¾ mile landscaped path to the Shrine.

The Shrine of La Virgen de San Juan del Valle is open daily with scheduled Mass times, although visitors and pilgrims are welcome at any time. Check the website or call for scheduled events.

FAMOUS PEOPLE IN TEXAS

SAM HOUSTON

Babe Didrikson Zaharias Museum
1750 E. IH-10
Beaumont, TX 77704
(409) 833-4622
http://www.babedidriksonzaharias.org/museum.cfm

Born Mildred Didrikson, the Babe is best known for her golfing ability. However, golf was far from being her only talent. Nicknamed after Babe Ruth for her sandlot baseball playing as a child, Didrikson "sports" quite a bit on her resume: basketball, javelin, hurdles, high jump, swimming, football (halfback), billiards, tumbling, boxing, wrestling, fencing, weight lifting, tennis, diving, adagio dancing and of course, baseball and golf. In addition, she played harmonica on Vaudeville and won the 1931 Texas State Fair sewing competition. She was truly among the outstanding women in Texas.

Babe broke a number of track and field world records in 1932 competing in the Amateur Athletic Union Championships as well as the Olympics in Los Angeles. Afterwards, in her 20's, Babe discovered golf. It proved to be a lifelong love of hers, winning 82 golf tournaments in her 23 years of playing. Babe died in Galveston in 1956 from colon cancer that had spread to her lymph nodes.

The Babe Didrikson Zaharias Museum couples as the Beaumont Visitors Center. The 16 glass panels that display her life may seem small, but they hold the memory of an athletic giant. The willing curators of the museum share a wealth of information about the Babe, as well as southeast Texas. Other memorabilia include a set of golf clubs, trophies, newspaper clippings, plaques, certificates, photographs, gloves, and balls.

Outside, twin fountains frame the entrance to the museum, and opens up to the Babe D. Zaharias Park. A number of soccer fields sprinkle the park, along with a 1.4 mile jogging trail. A playground, suspension bridge, USAF jet plane and Challenger memorial top off the park's attractions— all of which would make, in her own words, the "greatest athlete who ever lived" happy to see her memory fostering physical activity and personal greatness.

The museum is open 9:00 a.m. to 5:00 p.m. daily, except for Christmas Day, and is wheelchair accessible. Babe is buried a few miles away from the museum in Forest Lawn Memorial Park. Her gravesite includes a marker from the Texas Historical Commission as being an Outstanding Woman of Texas.

TEXAS FUN FACT:

Babe Didrikson went to Beaumont High School with the author's grandmother, Mariella Covington Taylor.

Brookshire's World of Wildlife Museum and Country Store
1600 WSW Loop 323
Tyler, TX
(903) 534-2169
www.brookshires.com/museum

Brookshire Brother's Grocery opened their first store in 1921, led by brothers Austin and Tom. Eight brothers and sisters joined by 1928, including Wood T. and his wife, Louise. By 1939, the "brother" count was reduced to 4, and the company split to divide responsibilities. Wood T. and Louise stayed in the Tyler area, and the Brookshire Brothers grocery stores prospered. Brookshire Brothers went corporate in 1962, growing to 61 stores by 1990.

As Brookshire Brother's, Inc. profited, Wood T. and Louise found themselves with the opportunity to explore the world; their specific interest focused in Africa. They wanted to share these experiences with others, to help expand appreciation for the animals in the land. They went on safari, and brought back animal trophies for display. Three trips between 1967 and 1971 provided many animals; so in 1975, part of the original corporate building was converted into a Wildlife and General Store Museum. By 1990, a larger building was purchased, and then expanded in 2004 to encompass added community donations.

At first approach to the museum grounds, visitors are greeted by giraffe, elephants, and rhino replicas. While unusual, it is only the beginning. Guests are provided with a self-guided tour pamphlet and a short informational talk about the museum. After walking through the glass doors, visitors are almost immediately surrounded by animals. First, through the North American room of bears, coyotes, and moose, visitors quickly see past the close proximity of the creatures to understand Wood T. and Louise's vision. The Brookshires have given children the up-front opportunity to experience the animals safely. Standing next to a polar bear is clearly the way to understand the vastness of the beast; an active imagination brings appreciation quickly. So, it's off to Africa, for the lion, zebra, and real giraffe.

The Brookshire World of Wildlife Museum has over 450 animals, aquatic and land, African and North American. Close to the end of the inside tour, visitors can walk straight into a 1920's country store. The Brookshires chose the 20's example, with period tools and food displays for a similar reason as why they provided the animal exhibits—to experience something different so that our own lives can be appreciated. Through the country store, Wood T. shows what people went through to get where we are today. While state-of-the-art in the 20's, the wood and metal meat slicer or peanut roasting machine may seem old-fashioned, even primitive, by today's standards. Yet, these tools and many more show the growth of the grocery industry in the past century.

Just as children have the chance to use their minds inside Brookshire's World of Wildlife, they can use their bodies outside in the park and picnic area of the museum. A 1952 LaFrance fire truck, used by the Dallas and Grand Saline Fire Departments, is a favorite climb-over, as its smiling face welcomes all who wish to scramble around its shiny red body. A restored railroad "Prune Peddler's Choo-Choo" caboose and a 1926 McCormick Deering farm tractor join in the fun as well. Sticking with the theme of the park, replicas of two giant tortoises and an American alligator are also included. Families often enjoy picnic lunches after a morning of gaining appreciation for things and beings they may not have experienced before. Mr. and Mrs. Brookshire's intentions are clear, and live on in the museum.

The Brookshire's World of Wildlife Museum and Country Store is open Tuesday through Saturday. From March 1st to September 30th, operating hours are 9:00 a.m. to 5:00 p.m.; they are open from 10:00 a.m. until 4:00 p.m. for the remainder of the year.

Conrad Hilton Museum

309 Conrad Hilton

Cisco, TX 76437

(254) 442-2537

www.ciscotx.com/chamber.htm

www.ciscotx.com/ciscopd/conradhilton.html

Conrad Hilton was born Christmas Day in 1887 to August and Mary Hilton in San Antonio, New Mexico Territory. "Connie" was raised as one of eight Hilton children, learning two valuable lessons from their parents. The first—work hard, and that he did, learning from doing whatever necessary to help the family business. (He even carried luggage from the train station to the rented rooms in their house when the family was tight on money). The second lesson he learned, from his mother, was *pray*. These two things took Conrad Hilton far in his lifetime. So far, that few can hear his name and not think of the empire he built that bears his name—Hilton Hotels.

In 1919, Conrad's father was killed in a car accident, and Conrad returned to the states after serving in France during World War I. Looking to make money in the booming oil industry, Hilton moved on to Cisco, a small Central Texas town, rich with oil. After a deal to buy the bank in Cisco fell through, Hilton noticed the nearby Mobley Hotel. It was amazing! Every eight hours, the hotel's guest list did a complete changeover, as shift workers returned to the oil mines for work. Hilton spoke with Mr. Mobley, and a few days later, the hotel was Hilton's. The success of the hotel in Cisco inspired Hilton to expand. He started in Fort Worth, through America, and eventually purchased hotels in other nations. Before Conrad Hilton's death in 1979, 185 stateside and 75 foreign hotels bore the Hilton name.

Hilton's 1919 Mobley purchase still stands in Cisco. It has served the community in many ways: hotel, boarding house, nursing home, private residence. It was even vacant a while until the Hilton Foundation dedicated $1.2 million to its restoration. The hotel now serves as the

Cisco Chamber of Commerce, multiple museums, two restored hotel rooms, a park, community center, and it is on the National Register of Historic Places. The museum exhibit "Innkeeper to the World" is devoted to the life of "Connie" Hilton, from his humble beginnings to the extravagance later in life. Visitors will learn about the stories behind his hotel acquisitions as well as the stories behind his charitable contributions. Life in Washington and life in Hollywood shaped Hilton's image, and the museum provides late-night talk show footage of Hilton from the 1950's and 60's, as a man with celebrity status. Through the while, he maintained his work ethic, fulfilling the true "American Dream".

The Cisco Chamber of Commerce and Conrad Hilton Museum are open Monday through Friday, 9:00 a.m. to noon and 1:00 p.m. until 5:00 p.m. Upstairs, visitors can tour the Cisco History Museum and learn how oil, water and railroads shaped Cisco as a town. Outside on the hotel lot, children enjoy a caboose-equipped playground, (while parents enjoy the "fenced-in" feature).

TEXAS FUN FACT:

Cisco is best known for the Santa Claus Bank Robbery—two days before Christmas 1927.

Edison Plaza Museum

350 Pine Street

Beaumont, TX 77701

(409) 981-3089

www.edisonmuseum.org

Although "America's Inventor" never visited Beaumont, Texans have the ability to recognize greatness when we see it! Thomas Alva Edison is honored in Beaumont's first downtown museum—the only museum dedicated to the inventor west of the Mississippi. Over 2,000 artifacts and related items are housed in the historic Travis Street Substation building. The Substation was the first to provide power to the farms in the Beaumont area in 1929, so it proves itself worthy of holding the history of the man who provided light to the world with his incandescent lamp invention in 1879.

Thomas Alva Edison is credited with 1093 patented inventions, including his first, the tin foil phonograph. This phonograph sparked his ideas for improvement, and he went on to later expand upon this concept in his life, developing such items as the telescribe and motion picture camera. Contrary to popular belief, Edison did not invent the light bulb; he only perfected it for practical, safe and economical widespread use by lowering the electrical current, adding the carbonized filament and improving the vacuum inside the now-known incandescent bulb. Other inventions include the steel alkaline battery and wireless communication devices for trains and ships.

The museum proudly boasts information about Edison and his creations Monday through Friday, 9:00 a.m. to 5:00 p.m. They are closed on holidays. Reservations are not required, but are recommended.

Elisabet Ney Museum in Hyde Park

304 East 44th Street

Austin, TX 78751

(512) 458-2255

www.ci.austin.tx.us/elisabetney

Elisabet Ney, a true Texan revolutionary, came to America in 1870 sharing her ideas of how art and beauty are intertwined with the shaping of a nation and its individuals.

Against her family's wishes, Ney chose to pursue the life of an artist, attending art academies in Munich and Berlin. She developed great skill as a sculptor, and went on to create marble portraits of prominent European personalities, including philosopher Arthur Schopenhauer, writer Jacob Grimm, Kings Ludwig II of Bavaria and George V of Hanover, and King George's court concert master, Josef Joachim. While sculpting her subjects, they became much more than that to her; she invested herself in each as individuals. By taking the time to know the person, her art shows not only the physical attributes, but spirit as well.

In 1892, Ney was commissioned to create life-sized portrait sculptures of Sam Houston and Stephen F. Austin for the 1893 World Fair in Chicago. These sculptures are now in the Texas State Capitol building. Ney enjoyed the city of Austin, and built a home that she called *Formosa*, (Portuguese for "beautiful") in 1892. *Formosa* became the center for legendary gatherings in Texas, proving Ney's theory of the close ties between art and power.

After her death in 1907, her friends purchased the house and founded the Elisabet Ney Museum as well as the Texas Fine Arts Association. Despite the constant sponsorship of exhibits and programs, they could not keep up with the property, and it was assumed by the City of Austin in 1941. However, the spirit of Ney lives on, as visitors enjoy her work and the castle-like limestone home. The crested tower, complete with hidden door, tops the classical and romantic type architecture. The museum holds 150 pieces of art by Ney—either original marble or plaster replicas of statues in other parts of the world (Ney has sculptures in the Smithsonian Museum of American Art and various European museums and royal palaces). Hyde Park surrounds the property now, and is a popular stop for picnickers and families.

Museum hours are Wednesday through Saturday, 10:00 a.m. to 5:00 p.m., and Sunday, noon to 5:00 p.m. The Elisabet Ney Museum is the only studio-museum of a 19th century professional woman sculptor working in America.

TEXAS FUN FACT:

Austin is considered the live music capital of the world

George Paul Museum

810 South Main St.

Del Rio, TX 78840

(830) 775-9595

www.georgepaulbullriding.com

George Paul was born March 4, 1947, and lived the life of a rancher and cowboy from an early age. Growing up on the San Miguel Ranch in Mexico, he rode anything on the grounds that tried him otherwise. The hero of his childhood? That would be Stoney Burke, a television character played by Jack Lord based on the life of real rodeo champion Casey Tibbs. No matter what, Stoney went after the championship. George Paul found a bit of himself in the old television show; he, too, would stop at nothing to earn the title of World Champion Bull Rider.

By 1966, George had joined the American Junior Rodeo Association, earned the World Championship in Bareback Bronc Riding, the Bull Riding title, and All-Around Cowboy award. He then refined his skills, attended the Jim Shoulders Rodeo School, and by 1967, he entered every rodeo he could wrap his feet around. He racked up the points, earning championship honors along the way. Once, he even competed in three different states' rodeos in one day! Traveling by land was quite cumbersome, so George took to the air in 1968, piloting his own twin engine Bonanza over 125,000 miles in the 150 rodeos in which he competed. The last half of the season brought George to world record status—by the time he entered the National Finals Rodeo, he had consecutively and successfully ridden 79 bulls. The first bull of the NFR, Cowtown, brought an end to his streak, but his record is a feat not touched by another before or since.

After winning the World Championship that year, George decided to stay home and help run the family ranch. He couldn't stay gone for long, though, and in 1970, the rodeo bug had bitten him again. However, this time, the sport in which George dedicated his life, took it. His plane crashed near Kemmerer, Wyoming, on a trip between rodeos. George was 23 years old when he died.

Since George's passing, professional rodeo bull riding is now considered an independent sport, and it's easy to see how George's life influenced this. His family and friends hold an annual George Paul Memorial Bull Riding in Del Rio, George's birthplace, to commemorate his life. Del Rio is also host to the George Paul Museum and Gift Shop, where visitors can learn about the life and legacy of this great bull rider. The museum, although small in its beginnings, shares photographs, clothing items, saddles, award buckles, and more of George's belongings. Particular items of interest are his trademark vests, and photos of George and singer Tom Jones from the family ranch in Mexico. A propeller from George's plane is also on display, found by in 2006 by John Ludlum, long-time family friend of the Pauls.

The George Paul Museum is run by Ludlum and George's brother, Bobby Paul. Jackie Sorrell, Bobby's daughter, manages the gift shop as well as the goings-on with the memorial bull riding event. They are housed in the historic Big Country Saddlery building, appropriate for George's story, although the saddle shop is long since gone. The museum and gift shop are open Tuesday through Friday, 10:00 a.m. to 6:00 p.m., and Saturday 10:00 a.m. until 4:00 p.m. Guests are welcome any time, but please call ahead to make sure John or Bobby is available for a guided tour. Each provide nice insight to George as a person, and share the love his family and friends have for this great bull riding cowboy.

TEXAS FUN FACT:

Texas is home to Dell and Compaq computers and Central Texas is often referred to as the Silicon Valley of the south.

Haley Memorial Library and History Center

1805 W. Indiana

Midland, TX 79701

(432) 682-5785

www.haleylibrary.com

Although Midland is popular nowadays as the home of President George W. Bush and First Lady Laura Bush, the town also has an older son, dedicated to the preservation of the history and traditions of the Frontier. James Evetts Haley wrote more than twenty books and uncountable articles/editorials about the American Southwest. He understood the effect of understanding our history and its impact on our future, and devoted much of his life to accounting the lives and events that shaped the southwest region.

Haley founded the Memorial Library and History Center in 1961, dedicated to the memory of his wife, Nita. The current building opened in 1976. Inside, it houses more than 25,000 items—books, papers, manuscripts, photographs and more—documenting life in the southwest ranching era. Among the collection are writing works by J. Evetts Haley, including *Charles Goodnight: Cowman and Plainsman*, a publication continuously in print since first released in 1936. Other books include 1952's *Fort Concho and the Texas Frontier*, and *Jeff Milton, a Good Man with a Gun* from 1948. Haley's ability to paint a true picture of life in young Texas is second to none, evidenced by the number of authors who consult his works when looking for that glimpse into our state's past.

To enhance the extensive research facility, the HMLRC contains numerous works of art from and about the "Wild West". As many collectors, Haley appreciated the connection between art as an integral piece in understanding a historical era. Realistic and impressionistic works are treasured links to the past. The HMLRC shares glass ware, pottery, baskets, blankets, saddles, firearms, and western gear—not just as relics, but artistic pieces. An original Alamo mission bell, cast in 1722, shines as a treasured piece. Illustrations by Harold Bugbee, Joe Beeler and others, as well as paintings by Bob Lougheed and William Meyers depict ranch life. Visitors find "Old Maude" a favorite. The life-sized bronze longhorn cow and her calf by Veryl Goodnight greet researchers and tourists, welcoming them into times past.

The Haley Memorial Library and Research Center is open Monday through Friday, 9:00 a.m. to 5:00 p.m. While in the area, visitors may want to stop by the Museum of the Southwest (one block north on S. K, and another block east on Missouri at 1805 W. Indiana). As the name implies, the Museum of the Southwest shares a mission with the HMLRC—to preserve the history of the southwest through art. Housed in the historic Turner Mansion, MSW has an extensive collection of southwestern artists, from period to contemporary. Hand colored lithographs by John Woodhouse Audubon, paintings by Taos Society Artists, and engravings by Karl Bodmer contribute to the permanent collection, while the museum also hosts a number of traveling exhibits as well. The museum also has a children's museum and planetarium that require tickets, but the art collection is free and a nice extension to the Haley Memorial Library and Research Center. Call or see the Museum of the Southwest's website for details and directions. (432) 682-5785 or www.museumsw.org.

TEXAS FUN FACT:

An average of 123 tornadoes touch down in Texas each year

John Nance Garner Museum
The Center for American History
333 North Park Street
Uvalde, TX 78801
(830) 278-5018
www.cah.utexas.edu/museums/garner_intro.php

John Nance Garner, known as "Cactus Jack" was one of the most influential and powerful vice presidents in American history. His keen observation skills led to his growth into a wily, cunning lawmaker, while his boisterous personality added to his "persuasive tactics" made him quite memorable not only as a Son of Texas, but as a United States politician.

Garner was born in 1868 in Detroit, Texas, and first came to Uvalde in 1892 to practice law after his schooling in Clarksville. By 1893, he served as county judge, and 1898, he was elected to the state legislature. He entered the 15th Congressional District (a position he helped establish) in 1903, and served 15 consecutive terms until 1933 when he transitioned into the second most powerful position in U.S. government- the vice presidency.

Garner served as vice president under Franklin D. Roosevelt. From partnership beginnings, they did not completely agree, but still presented ideas as a team effort (although Garner never hid his opinions). As Roosevelt's New Deal moved more towards welfare state concepts, he and Garner began to split—politically and in friendship. This increased distrust in Roosevelt led to Garner's blanket opposition, eventually leading to the New Deal demise. The end of Garner's second term as vice president inspired him to run for top office, but he was voted out in the primary elections. It was time for "Cactus Jack" to go home.

Garner spent the rest of his life in Uvalde; it was close to 30 years before he died in 1967, a few days shy of his 99th birthday. After his wife, Ettie, died, he moved out of the North Park Street home, donating it to the city to use as a museum in memory of Ettie. This home is now the John Nance Garner Museum, one of four divisions of the University of Texas' Center for American History. The museum documents the lives of both Cactus Jack and Ettie.

UTCAH's John Nance Garner Museum is roughly divided into two halves. Upon entering the old home, visitors can learn about the former vice president's personal life on the right, and his political career on the left. The back of the home displays temporary regional exhibits, often dealing with specific areas of interest either to Uvalde or Garner.

Garner's personal life exhibit displays items from his home, family photographs and a period kitchen. The kitchen also has memorabilia from Uvalde Honey and the dedication plaque from Garner's original donation of the house as a museum. The professional exhibit displays photographs letters, political cartoons, and inaugural attire worn by Vice President and Mrs. Garner in 1933. A room off to the side shares Garner's hobbies as a sportsman and poker player (to name a few). Another item of interest includes the November 22, 1963 phone record from the Fort Worth hotel where President John F. Kennedy had stayed the night. He called Garner that morning with birthday wishes; it was the last phone call JFK made before his assassination later that day.

The University of Texas Center for American History John Nance Garner Museum is open 9:00 a.m. to 5:00 p.m., Tuesday through Saturday. It is closed Monday and major holidays. Garner's gravesite is in the Uvalde Cemetery off of US 90 (route is labeled). The site is on the right side of the cemetery (old section) and is marked with flag poles and a Texas Historical Marker.

TEXAS FUN FACT:

John Nance Garner was a major investor in the First State Bank of Uvalde in 1913. The bank is still in operation, and now serves not only as a financial institution, but an art museum as well.

Judge Roy Bean Center

US 90 W State Loop 25 at Torres Ave.

Langtry, TX 78871

(432) 291-3340

www.drchamber.com/play/attractions/bean.html

"The Law West of the Pecos", Judge Roy Bean, was appointed to his post in Vinegerroon by Pecos County officials in 1882, mainly to alleviate the 400-mile round trip Texas Rangers had to make from Fort Stockton each time they were called to enforce the law (which happened to be quite often in the unruly camp).

Two years later, Bean relocated to Eagle's Nest, renamed the town Langtry after his favorite English actress, Lillie Langtry, and ran the town through "The Jersey Lilly"—his combination saloon-courtroom-billiard parlor-jail. His style of justice kept him in trouble with county officials as well as the Texas Rangers; however, his fitting sentences kept order in the "Wild West" Texas town. Many fictionalized stories spread through Texas about the judge, but the true ones were usually the most outlandish. There is no record of his sentencing anyone to death, but he didn't think twice about banning a horse thief from the town with no money, no transportation, no food, with the nearest town hundreds of miles away. Hearing tales of Bean's unusual rulings, outlaws soon changed ways while in the vicinity. He worked from a single law book, an 1879 *Revised Statutes*, (which wasn't opened much).

Judge Roy Bean didn't always agree with the law put forth by the Texas Rangers. For one, he thought it silly to prevent a man from carrying a weapon, as long as it wasn't concealed. So, when a defendant appeared before him on gun carrying charges, he simply stated that the man was standing still; he couldn't "carry" anything as long as he wasn't moving. The Judge ruled him innocent and turned his back as the man walked away.

Other stories exist about Bean and his nonconformist ways, many of which are shared at the Judge Roy Bean Visitor Center in Langtry. The center is 60 miles west of Del Rio—a long drive, certainly, but worth the time if in the area. The Visitor Center is run by the Texas Department of Transportation as a Travel Information Center. The large facility offers travel information about areas throughout the state, and friendly counselors are available to suggest routes and sites. Towards the back of the building, facts and "3-D" video kiosks about Vinegarroon, the local railroad, the High Bridge, Lillie Langtry, Bean's Prize Fight arrangement, and the judgments and other stories about Bean himself are available. An air conditioned video room shows a short film about the history of Bean and Langtry. A few of the judge's possessions are also available for viewing, including the 1879 law book, his personal gun, handcuffs, and his walking stick.

Outside, on the center grounds, visitors can walk around the center of old Langtry. "The Jersey Lilly" has photos, information and period furniture, as well as original signs from Judge Roy Bean's time of service. It was in this saloon that Bean died in 1903. The "Opera House" is also available to tour—the judge's home, named such to encourage a visit from Bean's secret love, Lillie Langtry. She did visit, in 1904, only months after Bean's death. A landscaped cactus garden completes the grounds, and is an incredibly informative display of native cactus. A descriptive brochure tells about each cactus, labeled both in the leaflet as well by the plant itself.

The Judge Roy Bean Visitor Center is open daily from 8:00 a.m. until 5:00 p.m. They are closed New Year's Day, Easter, Thanksgiving, and Christmas Eve and Day. Across the street at the community center, there is free dry-dock RV parking. After visiting the center, a drive around the area can provide tourists with stops at various Texas Historical Marker sites. Many include information about Judge Roy Bean and Langtry, marking places of interest and historical significance. The dirt road path also leads the way to the canyons of the Rio Grande. Ask a Texas Travel Information Center counselor for directions before leaving the center.

Light Crust Doughboys Hall of Fame and Museum

P.O. Box 767

Hwy. 37 at Jim Hogg Park

Quitman, TX 75783

(903) 763-2701

www.quitmanheritage.org/lightcrustdoughboys.htm

"The Light Crust Doughboys are on the air!" This announcement was known throughout the south in the 1930's as the introduction to the daily radio show spotlighting Texas' founding fathers of Western Swing. The band is not as well known now as in days gone by, but nevertheless continues on as the world's longest running country band.

The fiddling group was started in 1929 by Bob Wills as Wills Fiddle Band. With their sponsorship from Light Crust Flour that landed them a daily spot on live radio, the name changed to Light Crust Doughboys. After two weeks on the air, the general manager of the mill, W. Lee "Pappy" O'Daniel, cancelled the show, for personal dislike of the "hillbilly music". After some urging (and an agreement for the boys to work in the mill), the Light Crust Doughboys were back on the air.

Original band members started leaving the band in 1932 for various reasons, but O'Daniel quickly found replacements and the popular fiddling, swing style continued. By the early 1940's, their show was broadcast on over 170 radio stations. Through the decades, the Light Crust Doughboys gave hope and enjoyment to people, helping to forget about the economic problems of the Great Depression. The show stopped in 1942, but the Doughboys continue singing and playing still today. Front man Art Greenhaw now leads the group. Numbers and instruments fluctuate according to needs and audiences, but the Texas Swing can get just about anyone's toes tapping, just like in the good ol' days.

The Quitman Heritage Foundation proudly hosts the Light Crust Doughboy Hall of Fame and Museum, on the property of the Governor

Jim Hogg City Park on Highway 37. Numerous items are available for viewing, including instruments used by the band, promotional posters, and even packages of Light Crust Flour. Hogg City Park has a nature trail and shaded picnic areas, as well as historical homes and the "Miss Ima Hogg Museum". There is a small fee for visiting these other attractions. The Light Crust Doughboy Hall of Fame and Museum is open 9:00 a.m. until 4:00 p.m., Monday through Saturday, and is closed noon to 1:00 p.m. for lunch.

TEXAS FUN FACT:

Later in his career, William Lee "Pappy" O'Daniel was elected Governor of Texas and then U.S. Texas Senator, and was the only person to ever defeat Lyndon B. Johnson in a political race. When asked, he attributed his popularity to his association with the Light Crust Doughboys.

TEXAS FUN FACT:

A fictionalized "Pappy" O'Daniel with the first name of Menelaus was characterized in the Coen Brothers' film "*O, Brother, Where Art Thou?*" Although O'Daniel never involved himself in Mississippi politics, his reputation and personality made him a shoe-in character of the incumbent governor.

Lyndon B. Johnson National Historic Park

PO Box 329

Johnson City, TX 78636

(830) 868-7128

www.nps.gov/lyjo

On November 22, 1963, Lyndon B. Johnson became the 36th President of the United States, after the assassination of John F. Kennedy. He was elected to serve another term in 1964, with 61% of the popular vote—the greatest percentage ever attained by a presidential candidate. Throughout his presidency, he spoke of a "Great Society", and visitors to the Hill Country can visualize what must have been in his mind as he spoke of a country with clean air, clean water, good educational facilities, and a sense of belonging.

Johnson City visitors will see the boyhood home of our former president. His mother, Rebekah, a graduate of now-known University of Mary-Hardin Baylor, was one of the few college-educated women in the area. His father, Sam, was a state legislator. Both developed the strong family ties and sense of place—of being—the president held dear, apparent though his own legislation. Down a walking trail from the 9th Street home is the Johnson Settlement, land owned by LBJ's grandfather, Sam Ealy Johnson, Sr., and Sam's brother, Tom. LBJ's pride in the land that raised him guided his decision to donate funds to purchase the Johnson Settlement for preservation by the National Park Service. The Settlement includes an exhibit center, barns, the Johnson cabin, and of course, an education building.

Picturesque trees shade the flowered Johnson City National Park Visitor center, the former LBJ hospital. Inside, a wealth of knowledge is shared about the 36th president, including a timeline of his life and family, and accomplishments through his political career. Lady Bird, his wife, is also featured in the museum for her contributions to the preservation of wildlife and natural areas.

Down the road in Stonewall, is an additional National Park dedicated to LBJ's life. Lady Bird's love of wildflowers is apparent throughout the park by the Pedernales River, encompassing the statue area of LBJ in his "teacher pose". Some say Johnson points to the river where he spent many days; others say it's the Texas White House Complex inside the ranch. Either way, he points to home, an important place in the heart of this man.

Attached to the LBJ state park (see Sauer-Beckmann Living History Farm in Farms and Gardens section), the Stonewall National Park offers tours of LBJ's ranch. There is a transportation fee for the bus tour that goes into the ranch, however, from 5:00 p.m. until dark, visitors are able to drive down Park Road 49 to see Junction School, LBJ's reconstructed birthplace, home of Sam Ealy Johnson, Sr., the Cedar Guest House, and the breathtaking Johnson Family Cemetery. Scheduled school groups can request a waiver for the bus fees; the buses are free of charge August 27th (LBJ's birthday) and other designated days.

The Johnson City Visitor Center is open 8:45 a.m. until 5:00 p.m. daily, except Thanksgiving Day, Christmas Day, and New Year's Day. The Stonewall Visitor Center opens at 9:00 a.m. The LBJ National Park participates in the Junior Ranger program and has a park-specific curriculum for LBJ.

TEXAS FUN FACT:

In 1905, LBJ's father, Sam Johnson, a State legislator, was instrumental in appropriating funds to purchase the land around the Alamo for use as a National Monument.

Mary Kay Museum

16251 Dallas Parkway

Addison, TX

(972) 687-5720

www.marykay.com

Born in 1918, Mary Kathlyn Wagner grew up in Houston, caring for her sick father while her mother worked long hours. All the while, Mary Kathlyn maintained straight-A's, and consistently outsold other Girl Scouts in cookie sales. She often attributed her driving work ethic to her mother's "you can do it" attitude; she believed in Mary from the beginning. The confidence she gave her daughter would eventually spread throughout the United States.

Mary Kay grew up with intentions for medical school. When she discovered that her sales ability exceeded her science skills, her mind and career changed to sales. After 25 years of earning "top salesperson", Mary Kay retired. A month after retiring, she began to write a how-to book for career women. Her writing spawned the idea of starting her own business, and "Beauty by Mary Kay" was launched in 1963. Today, Mary Kay is one of the largest private firms in the United States, based on Mary's can-do attitude and system of recognition, motivation and support.

The Mary Kay Museum highlights the life and business history of Mary Kay Ash and her beauty products. Visitors are welcomed into the pink palace to a shrine of products, photographs (including some of Mary Kay's personal collection), awards, video clips, personal evening gowns, and collector's items. Mary Kay was exceptionally proud of receiving the Horatio Alger Award in 1978, honored for her "success in spite of adversity", and the award holds a special place of honor in the museum. Mary Kay also pays respect to those who helped make the company the success it is today in the "Keepers of the Dream" Hall of Honor. Sales leader portraits line the walls, faces of women who, through Mary Kay

Ash, lived with the "can-do" attitude. At the time of her death in 2001, Mary Kay's company made it possible for over 150 women to earn over $1 million in sales commissions, and more than 10,000 pink Cadillacs were awarded.

Mary's mother would be proud.

The Mary Kay Museum is open for self guided tours 9:00 a.m. until 4:30 p.m. Monday through Friday. Guided tours are available at 10:00 a.m. and 2:00 p.m., but must be scheduled at least three days in advance. The museum is closed on all major holidays.

Visitors who can't get enough of the Mary Kay industry are invited to visit the manufacturing facility 14 miles south of the headquarters building between I-35 and Hwy. 183. Reservations are necessary (same number as museum). Tour times are: Monday—2:00 p.m. Tuesday/Thursday—10:30 a.m. and 2:00 p.m. Friday—10:30 a.m.

TEXAS FUN FACT:

Pink was not Mary Kay's favorite color! Popular opinion showed that pink "looks good" with black and white—a common bathroom combination at the time. The color was chosen to encourage women to leave products out on display in the bathroom, further boosting self image. (A visit to the museum will reveal Mary Kay's color preference).

O. Henry House and Museum

409 East Fifth St.

Austin, TX 78701

(512) 472-1903

Born William Sydney Porter in North Carolina, the "Master of the Short Story" is best known as O. Henry. Porter spent 13 years in Austin where he met his wife, Athol, befriended the Driskill Brothers (of the Driskill Hotel fame), and witnessed the laying of the Capitol building's cornerstone in 1885. As a writer, Porter also held an assortment of other jobs, including the bookkeeping position at the First National Bank of Austin, where Porter was accused of embezzlement in 1897. He was tried, convicted, and spent 3 years in prison, after which he began writing under the name O. Henry. The house was originally on East Cedar and moved twice before being placed at its present location on 5th Street.

Visitors to the O. Henry house can browse through the author's former home and see personal items of Porter and his wife, including rare books, original furniture, photographs, and Porter's writing desk. The house is open Wednesday through Sunday noon until 5:00 p.m. A walking tour map, "The O. Henry Trail", is available through the Austin Convention and Visitors Bureau on historic 6th street. The map notes buildings of significance not only to O. Henry's life, but integral to Austin's history as well.

O. Henry is best known for his works "The Gift of the Magi" and "The Ransom of Red Chief". The twisted plots, irony and wordplay he created have kept readers on their toes for years. In his memory, the annual O. Henry Pun-Off (also free) is held on the property behind the museum each year in May. Crowds gather around the stage on blankets and chairs to delightfully groan at the wit and wisdom of contestants.

His legacy has proven to be a work of heart.

Sam Houston Memorial Museum Complex

1402 19th Street

Huntsville, TX 77340

(936) 294-1832

http://www.samhouston.memorial.museum

Sam Houston is an integral part of the history of the Lone Star State. Raised by Cherokee Indians in Tennessee, "the Raven" brought his pride and sense of justice and honor to Texas in the 1830's. The Sam Houston Memorial Museum gives insight into the life of the Republic of Texas' first president.

Visitors to the museum will find not only a single building about Sam Houston's life, but an entire park dedicated to his honor. The main museum offers information about Houston and the Republic of Texas, while the park includes buildings used by Sam and his family. Structures include his law office, a kitchen, and the family's woodland home from when Houston was governor of Texas. The blacksmith shop on the grounds frequently hosts demonstrations on the making of frontier tools, and there is a small lake—Oolooteca—named after Houston's adoptive Cherokee father. Local university art students often find inspiration here to sketch and paint.

The "Steamboat House," designed and built by Dr. Rufus Bailey, is also on the park site. After refusing to take the Confederate oath of allegiance, Sam Houston resigned as governor and moved into the Steamboat House with his family in 1862. In 1863, he died here of pneumonia.

An additional on-site exhibit hall shares highlights of the 19th century not covered in the main museum. The museum and historical buildings are open Tuesday through Saturday, 9:00 a.m. to 4:30 p.m., and Sunday noon to 4:30 p.m. The museum hosts a variety of educational programs as well as the General Sam Houston Folk Festival in April. Call or visit website for details.

While in Huntsville, visitors can also schedule a stopover at the Sam Houston Statue—the world's tallest statue of an American hero, standing at an amazing 67 feet tall. For more information, visit www.samhoustonstatue.org.

TEXAS FUN FACT:

The author, Tab Lloyd, attended SHSU in the early 1990's.

Sid Richardson Museum

309 Main Street

Fort Worth, TX 76102

(817) 332-6554

www.sidrichardsonmuseum.org

Sid Richardson was born in Athens, Texas in 1891, and grew up to find his fortune in the oil industry, like many others in the land. Sid loved Texas—her land, her people, her stories, and her artists. He took that love and put it to good use; he operated three cattle ranches, ran a radio/television station, owned a carbon plant, and financially backed a fellow Texan (for $20 million) fighting for control of the New York Central Railroad.

Throughout it all, "Mr. Sid" as he came to be known, did not enjoy the limelight, so the public was not aware of most of his endeavors. He made regular donations to civic groups, churches, libraries, hospitals, schools, and youth organizations. By 1950, Mr. Sid was considered one of the wealthiest men in the United States; his net worth was close to $800 million.

Mr. Sid began collecting art in 1942. His passion for all things Texas leaned his preferences towards western artists Frederic Remington and Charles Russell. Initially assisted by the Bertram Newhouse Galleries in New York, Richardson eventually collected 52 pieces from the two artists before his death in 1959. The Sid Richardson Foundation continues Mr. Sid's philanthropy today.

The Sid Richardson Museum opened in 1982 in a replica of an 1895 building. The Museum provides free educational programs for children and adults, including guided museum tours, on-site visits to schools and other institutions, and "second Saturday" tours, that provide background and stories specific to pieces in the galleries. The museum collections have extended to encompass more than just Remington and Russell, but continue to reflect the romantic legends of the Wild West. Visitors will find no landscapes here, but action-packed paintings depicting the character types Mr. Sid loved. The self guided brochures are an excellent resource, sharing personal stories about the artists, the specific piece (subject and history), and suggested artistic interpretations.

The Sid Richardson Museum is open daily: Monday through Thursday, 9:00 a.m. to 5:00 p.m., Friday and Saturday, 9:00 a.m. to 8:00 p.m., and Sunday noon-5:00 p.m.; they are closed on major holidays. The online website provides a number of resources, including suggested reading lists about the artists and visiting museums with children, educator guides, and a 10-lesson "Art and Archives" program enabling teachers to bring the Wild West experience into classrooms.

Around the corner at Commerce and 2nd street, is the "150 Years of Fort Worth" museum, housed in the 1907 Fire Station No. 1. The building is the site of Fort Worth's original city hall: city offices upstairs, volunteer firefighters (and their cougar mascot, "Bill") downstairs. The building originally reopened as the museum as part of Texas' sesquicentennial celebration, but continues on many years past to share the city's story. The 150 Years of Fort Worth is open daily from 9:00 a.m. until 8:00 p.m.

TEXAS FUN FACT:

The 2,500-acre Sid Richardson Scout Ranch by Lake Bridgeport provides a number of experiences for Boy Scouts through the extensive facilities and land formations. The ranch is utilized throughout the year by Cub Scout Packs, Boy Scout Troops, and Venturing Crews for camps and programs through the Boy Scouts of America.

TEXAS FUN FACT:

In 1873, the *Dallas Herald* competitively printed that Fort Worth was so boring that a panther (A.K.A. cougar or mountain lion) was seen sleeping by the courthouse. Fort Worth retaliated by embracing the animal as its mascot. In 1875, the Trinity River overflowed, and forced a real cougar into town; this one did not sleep, but roamed the streets (startling a few citizens) before returning home. The "sleepy little town" has been awake ever since.

TRADE

5 D Custom Hats & Leather

742-A Butternut

Abilene, TX 79602

(325) 673-9000

www.5dhats.com

Texas is steeped in tradition, and Abilene is no exception. Visitors will enjoy that traditional feel at 5 D Custom Hats, mixed up with a good dose of country humor.

Damon Albus didn't start off in the hat making business, but he has certainly found his niche there. After graduating from Tarleton State University, he spent a few years in the criminal justice field, only to find something pulling him back home to Abilene. Interested in leatherwork and hand crafts, Damon learned the trade of custom hat making, and opened his store in 1997. The name "5 D" originally came from the family brand of his youth, representing his parents and their three sons: Dwight, Donna, Darren, Dennis, and the youngest, Damon. Damon found a gal with the same name as his mom, and now the "5 D" tradition lives on in his own family with their children Delani, Dalli, and Dash.

In a time of mass production, 5 D Custom Hats works for the individual. "Custom" is returned to the customer, as heads are precisely measured for the exact style and fit desired, taking the "break-in" time out of a new hat. The craft of hat making is reminiscent of days-gone-by, and the tools used reflect that lost time. Much of 5 D's equipment is from the 1930's (and not made since), but the prized possessions that truly makes the business a custom hat shop are the conformer and extractor from 1895-1905—measuring tools that not only measure the circumference of a head, but the specific shape as well.

5 D prides itself on the quality of materials as well as the fit of a custom made hat. Beaver, rabbit and nutria fur blends are used to make all felt hats; no wool is used at all. Sweatbands are machine-sewn, but hand stitched into the hat by Donna after Damon shapes and molds the hat to

customer preferences. Add a trim, and "yee-haw", the hat is ready to go, no matter if the hat is special occasion attire or the staple of a daily wardrobe.

Businessmen to rodeo champions—and everyone in-between—wear 5 D Custom Hats. Larry Hagman, Joe Beaver, Guy Allen, Allen Bach, and Jim Davis are a few of the better known 5 D wearers; many more sport their hats with pride (even when they're not supposed to!). 5 D is happy to show visitors around the store and production area, eager to share the entire process and answer any questions. Even those who don't particularly fancy "cowboy" hats can find time well spent learning about this historic trade and sharing a few laughs with the 5 D family. However, if the start-to-finish, "super-deluxe" tour is wanted, call ahead. Damon is happy to do it himself—if, of course, you bring him a Dr. Pepper.

TEXAS FUN FACT:

The official "state sport" of Texas is rodeo.

Breedlove Dehydrated Foods

1818 North Martin Luther King Blvd.

Lubbock, TX 79403

(806) 741-0404

www.breedlove.org

Breedlove Dehydrated Foods opened in 1983 and is the largest dehydration plant in the world. The dehydration process, interesting as it may be, is not what makes Breedlove special. Breedlove *gives* their food away, making them the largest charity food bank in the world, according to the Guinness Book of World Records (first recognized in 1996).

Breedlove works as part of the International Food Relief Partnership (IFRP) and the United States Agency for International Development (USAID), using agricultural contributions that would otherwise be thrown away to make nourishing food products for people cannot provide food for themselves. Dehydrating the vegetables makes it easier and more cost-effective to transport and store the final products. A two-pound box of food can provide anywhere from 50-60 servings, and products usually have a shelf life of around two years.

Ninety percent of the food distributed by Breedlove is through hunger relief programs, and they ship to 55 different countries; Kenya, the Philippines, tsunami victims, and Katrina/Rita victims are some recipients. The food is usually coupled with other health related activities including hospitals and orphanages, to ensure the health and well being of each member of the needy community.

Visitors are welcome at Breedlove, as the company is committed not only to providing food staples to others, but education as well. Dehydration process tours are available, and include an eight minute video about Breedlove's part in USAID and IFRP. Awareness programs are also offered free of charge. They include "Hunger Banquet"—groups of 25 or more experience the dynamics of poverty, "Feed the Need"—an interactive program for students in grades 3-12 that includes a facility tour, and "Humble Lunch"—a lunchtime talk with a Breedlove worker while enjoying the company's products. The director is also flexible in creating a program to fit needs of Scout groups or other organizations. Tours and awareness programs are available 8:00 a.m. to 5:00 p.m. daily; however, please call to arrange times, to ensure the Program Director is available.

TEXAS FUN FACT:

There are 6736 lakes in Texas.

TEXAS FUN FACT:

The largest is the Sam Rayburn Reservoir, covering 113,400 acres in East Texas

Bureau of Engraving and Printing

9000 Blue Mound Rd.

Fort Worth, TX 76131

(800) 865-1194

www.moneyfactory.gov

The Bureau of Engraving and Printing was originally established in 1861; a handful of workers separated and sealed notes by hand in the U.S. Treasury basement. Things have changed through the years, and the Bureau now produces paper currency in two facilities—Washington, D.C. and Fort Worth, Texas. The Fort Worth Facility opened its doors in 1991 to meet the overwhelming need for currency production. Although the printing process has kept up with the technology of the times, the Bureau's engravers continue the use of the first artist tools: the graver, the burnisher, and hand held glass. Working to thwart counterfeiters, the BEP also is responsible for sections of U.S. passports, military ID cards, immigration and naturalization certificates, homeland security materials and various other U.S. security items.

Visitors to the BEP will have the opportunity to witness the creation of up to millions of dollars worth of notes during the visit. The 45-minute facility tour shows and explains the various steps of currency production as guests walk the quarter-mile, enclosed suspended walkway over the production floor. After (or before) touring the production room, a 15 minute informative film and numerous interactive exhibits share the history of currency and involved details of the printing process. A favorite spot is the "How Tall Are you Worth?" tower, where children and adults alike measure height in dollars. Visitors watch as workers demonstrate printing on the antique spider press and analyze mutilated money turned in for redemption.

The Bureau of Engraving and Printing is a secure facility. Guests are asked not to bring cell phones, electronic equipment, backpacks, cameras, weapons, food or drinks to the production tour of the facility. Tourists are welcome on a first-come, first serve basis, unless reservations are made. It is highly suggested that tourists arrive at least 30 minutes prior to tour time in order to clear security. August through May, the BEP Visitor Center is open 8:30 a.m. to 3:30 p.m.; tours start every thirty minutes from 9:00 a.m. until 2:00 p.m. In June and July, the center is open from 10:30 a.m. until 6:30 p.m.; tours begin every half hour from 11:00 a.m. until 5:00 p.m. The BEP is closed weekends, federal holidays and the week between December 25 and January 1. American Sign Language and Spanish interpreters are available upon request.

TEXAS FUN FACT:

Not surprisingly the "state dish" of Texas is chili. There is a long lived debate as to whether "true" Texas Chili has beans or not (but as all "true" Texans know, beans are a separate dish, and are NOT to be mixed with chili at all! Violators have known to be hanged for such deeds in the state's youth.)

The Candle Factory

4411 South IH 35

Georgetown, TX 78628

(512) 863-6025

www.thecandlefactory.com

Old Georgetown Candles, founded in 1967, started as a small, hand-dipped candle factory. The company grew, was sold to Ellen and Paul Nuckolls in 1987, and is now known as The Candle Factory. It is one of a handful of large factories in the United States that still hand produces candles.

The Candle Factory is known for their hand dipped tapers; however, the company does not stop there. In addition to the tapers, they manufacture machine made pillars, molded decorative pillars (quite extravagant), and numerous novelty candles. There are more than 300 types of candles, plus fifty colors and scents, which makes for a multitude of combinations!

Upon arrival, welcomed visitors walk into a fragrant production room, where workers dip the tapers into large vats of hot wax. If lucky, a delicate basket candle might be viewed as well (wicks woven into a cylindrical, bottomless basket shape and dipped in candle wax). Knowledgeable workers are happy to share information with visitors about the 100-year-old process.

In the showroom, tourists will see examples of each type of candle in production, including a selection of the 200+ shaped candles—"Angels to Giraffes to Zebras with a lot in between". Popular items also include shaped Alamos, Yellow Roses of Texas, and cow skulls. How about a buffalo chip? (No worries- that one's not scented!) The decorative pillars are extraordinary—sculpted roses, shell filled, or carved. All are worth the trip.

Guests may buy candles from the showroom or online, but purchase is not necessary to visit and tour the facility. Visitors are welcome seven days a week, but demonstrations are only given on weekdays. Call to set up a demonstration, to ensure availability. The factory and store are open Monday through Saturday, 9:00 a.m. to 5:30 p.m. and Sunday 10:00 a.m. to 5:30 p.m., and is closed only on New Year's Day, Easter, Thanksgiving, and Christmas Day.

TEXAS FUN FACT:

Extra bright specialty candles from The Candle Factory were featured in the movies THE ALAMO and SPY KIDS.

James Leddy Boots

1602 North Treadaway

Abilene, TX 79601-3011

(325) 677-7811

www.abilenevisitors.com/visitors/frontierheritagetour.html

Ever wonder why cowboys—the real ones—never, EVER take off their boots? It's because once they're worn in, they're like a second skin. Some say they feel incomplete, even lonely, without them. In our world of mass production and marketing, western boots are readily available, and made to fit everyone. Sure, they may not fit your foot or your taste exactly, but a customer can walk into a store, and walk out instantly with a new pair, however uncomfortable, on his or her feet. To men like James Leddy who take their footwear seriously, boots are a part of the Texan lifestyle, whether the wearer is working the ranch or doing the boot-scootin' boogie. Leddy's boot shop provides one thing the mass markets cannot: no break-in time and instant comfort. As everyone knows, a hard day's work is much easier in comfortable footwear. Custom made boots are James Leddy's business, and his business is good.

Mr. Leddy extends his hand to meet the foot of each customer. He measures carefully and questions for exact preferences. A price is agreed upon, as well as a time frame. The entire process, from measurement to "walk out wearing them" is completed within the little Abilene shop. Leather is cut, designed, embroidered, punched and sewn until a brand-new set of boots are born for the one and only feet for whom they were specifically designed.

Visitors to James Leddy Boots are welcome to drop in and watch the process any time during hours of operation. The craftsmen (and women) pleasantly answer questions, comfortable to share their skills in this long-lost art. If a more formal tour is desired, call ahead to arrange a time when an employee, or Mr. Leddy himself, can share the stories of his boot making career. There is a small display room with examples, books, and photographs of the footwear made in the shop; a careful look might notice a few famous faces: George Jones, Mel Tillis, and Jerry Lee Lewis to name a few. Whoever it might be—a famous singer, stylish dresser, or hard-working rancher, James Leddy Boots can provide a pair of boots as unique as their owner.

James Leddy Boots is open weekdays from 8:00 a.m. until 5:00 p.m. There is no website for the store itself. Please call for directions or to arrange a guided tour.

TEXAS FUN FACT:

The official "state flower" of Texas is the bluebonnet. Contrary to the popular myth it is not illegal to pick them.

Mrs. Baird's Bakery

Headquarters
14401 Statler Blvd.
Fort Worth, TX 76155
(817) 864-2500
www.mrsbairds.com

Mrs. Baird ("Ninnie"), born in Tennessee, found her way to Texas with her husband, William, in 1901. They moved to Fort Worth with four children, ready to continue the restaurant and bakery business started in their former state. William introduced the first steam popcorn machine to Fort Worth; it was an instant success. Investment in a second popcorn vending spot raised enough revenue for the Bairds' dream to come true. With the restaurant purchase, Ninnie became head baker and her reputation rose as quickly as her yeasted bread.

William developed diabetes and found it difficult to work, but his and Ninnie's eight children were there to help. The three oldest worked the restaurant and bakery, while the others helped run the household and care for their father. Ninnie baked continuously in her 4-loaf, wood burning stove, and realized that due to the popularity of her bread, her living could be made right there in her oven. She sold the restaurant in 1908, and founded Mrs. Baird's Bread. Mr. Baird passed away in 1911.

By 1915, Mrs. Baird's Bread was so successful; it began a string of upgrades. The company grew, developing not only the Fort Worth facilities, but expanding to other Texas cities as well: Dallas, Houston, Abilene, Lubbock, Victoria, Waco, Austin, and San Antonio. When Ninnie died in 1961, at the age of 92, Mrs. Baird's Bread had nine plants and over 2,500 employees, making it the largest independent family-owned bakery in the country. The Bakery is part of the Texas Business Hall of Fame (1992) and the Baking Hall of Fame (2006). Grupo Bimbo bought the company in 1998, creating Bimbo Bakeries USA.

Today, as throughout the years, Mrs. Baird's Bakeries provides tours for interested folks aged six and up. The tour begins with a short history of the Bakery and Ninnie Baird. Observing the process using computerized mixers, assembly lines, and mechanized tools, visitors can see how things are quite different from the 4-loaf wood burning stove bakery beginnings. Although much has changed, some things remain the same—important details that brought the success of the tasty Texas treat. The Mrs. Baird's Bread recipe has remained the same since 1908: flour, water, yeast, milk, and shortening. It's the same simple combination, just on a larger scale. Another constant is that each loaf of bread is hand-twisted, just as Ninnie did it, before its final rise and trip to the oven. After cooling, tourists can see the bread sliced and bagged, all within the blink of an eye. The best part of the tour comes at the end with a free sample of the product—warm, fresh and tasty. It's as if Ninnie handed it to you herself.

The Fort Worth Bakery is where it all started, and they offer the most tours, but the other facilities offer tours as well (see below). Reservations must be made at least 2 weeks in advance, and can be arranged through the website or calling the specific bakery. When touring the bakeries, please remember that the visits are scheduled for people over six years of age, legs must be covered, and they request no open toed shoes, jewelry, or video cameras. Before a trip, a virtual tour through the website will provide more information about the company's history, awards and products.

Fort Worth Bakery

7301 South Freeway

Fort Worth, TX 76134

(817) 615-3000

Tuesday through Thursday every hour from 10:00 a.m. until 4:00 p.m.

Houston Bakery
6650 N. Houston - Rosslyn Rd.
Houston, TX 77091
(713) 996-5000 x 5000

Wednesday and Thursday at 10:00 a.m. and 2:00 p.m.

San Antonio Bakery
512 South Gevers
San Antonio, TX 78203
(210) 533-5181

Thursday at 9:00 a.m. or 11:00 a.m.

Abilene Bakery
2701 Palm
Abilene, TX 79605
(325) 692-3141

Tours vary, contact office

Lubbock Bakery
202 E. Broadway
Lubbock, TX 79403
(806) 763-9304

Tuesday, Wednesday and Thursday mornings

Nokona Athletic Goods Company

208 Walnut Street

Nocona, TX 76255

(940) 825-3326

www.nokona.com

Nocona, Texas—named after Chief Peta Nocona, father of famed Chief Quanah Parker, was once known as the "Leather Capital of Texas. In 1926, noticing the success of local boot companies, Robert E. Storey purchased and operated a leather factory, specializing in wallets and purses. It proved a good investment; however, the strike of the Depression brought his business down quickly. Not wanting to quit, he searched for a new avenue, eventually settling on baseball mitts and sporting equipment.

Again, the business flourished, but like many things, the ups and downs come and go alternately. After years of success, the 1960's brought another challenge—many companies in the United States began producing out-of-country in order to bring prices down. Nocona Athletic Goods Company and the Storey family held steadfast to their principles; their products remain 100% American made to this day. Nocona concentrates on quality rather than quantity, and although priced on the high end of the market, Nocona gloves are prized by Baseball's best. Their fans include Nolan Ryan and John "Red" Murff.

Again, what goes up must come down. Nocona Athletic Goods Company's 1926 facility burned to the ground in July 2006. The resilient company recovered quickly, and was up and running again right at a year later, this time bringing in endorsements to help boost sales. The company may be in a new building, but the old standard remains. The major portion of each leather good is handmade, and a 100% American product.

Visitors are welcome to tour the new building and witness the precision and attention given to each piece of equipment. The total process of glove making is around 5 hours, but the knowledgeable tour guides share each step in much less time, from cutting to finished product, while sharing stories of the company's history. Tours are given Monday through Friday, 8:00 a.m. until 11:00 a.m. and 1:00 p.m. to 3:00 p.m. Anyone with special needs, please call ahead so that arrangements can be made.

TEXAS FUN FACT:

From 1836 to 1845, Texas was known as the Republic of Texas, and is the only state in the U.S. that has been an independent country. The annexation treaty agreeing to join the United States was approved under the Republic's 3rd elected president, Anson Jones.

Port of Houston Authority
Sam Houston Boat Tour

111 East Loop North

Houston, TX 77029

(713) 670-2400

http://www.portofhouston.com/samhou/samhou.html

The Port of Houston offers free 90-minute round trip tours of the ship channel aboard the *M/V Sam Houston*. Visitors on the 100 passenger boat can see a range of ships from all over the world, as well as oil refineries, barges, and tug boats, while learning about the trade and commerce of one of America's largest sea ports.

Since the *M/V Sam Houston*'s inauguration in 1958, more than a million passengers have found enjoyment and education on this trip. No food or beverages are allowed on the boat or in the Sam Houston Pavilion; however, complimentary soft drinks are provided for patrons half way through the ride.

Scheduled tours are: Tuesdays, Wednesdays, Fridays, and Saturdays- 10:00 a.m. and 2:30 p.m. Thursdays and Sundays host 2:30 p.m. trips only. Reservations are required, and tours can be cancelled without advance notice.

Texas Basket Company
100 Myrtle Drive

Jacksonville, TX 75766

(903) 586-8014 (800) 657-2200

www.texasbasket.com

Due to East Texas' rich soil and climate, fruits and vegetables quickly became the source of economic trade in the area. By the early 1900's, Tyler's peaches were quite popular, as were Jacksonville's tomatoes; Jacksonville became known as the "Tomato Capital of the World." The industry grew, and needed containers manufactured locally to meet the increasing shipping demand. So, in 1919, Texas Basket Company opened as a commercial basket manufacturer. Three other companies operated at the time, but Texas Basket Company is the only survivor from last century. It is locally owned and operated—has been since the beginning.

Texas Basket Company uses locally grown trees (within a 400-mile radius) to make baskets; a variety of trees are used, but sweetgum is the usual choice, due to its natural flexibility and resistance to production splitting. Logs are brought in, soaked, cut, assembled, dried, and shipped worldwide. Although the traditional fruit and vegetable baskets are popular, TBC has expanded business to meet needs and interests of customers. Shaped and painted gift-type baskets, art and craft supplies, and biodegradable nursery potting baskets are now on their product line.

Visitors can witness the factory process via observation room. Like many time-tested crafts, much of the machinery used at TBC dates before the 1940's. As time progressed, many produce farmers chose to discard baskets for less expensive cardboard boxes, so the basket making equipment is no longer made, making repairs a challenge. But Texas Basket Company has continued the traditional process, with much success. Texas Basket Company's gift shop is open Monday through Friday, 9:00 a.m. to 5:00 p.m. Visitors check here for the tour; best times for viewing are between 8:00 a.m. to 3:00 p.m., when the process is in full swing.

Wimberley Glass Works, Inc.

6469 Ranch Road 12

San Marcos, TX 78666

(800) 929-6686

www.wgw.com

Seven miles south of small-town Wimberley, area visitors find an unusually modern, bright yellow building off of Ranch Road 12. Home to Wimberley Glass Works, this building is the vision of Tim deJong, a relocated Canadian-born Texan. In New York, deJong studied ceramics, sculpture, and glass and he co-owned Carriage House Glass in Philadelphia, but a visit to Texas in 1991 gave him what he really wanted—an establishment where he could demonstrate his true artistic love of glassblowing.

The demonstration area at WGW gives visitors a first-hand look at the skill and concentration necessary to create the incredible pieces of functional, wearable or visual art (depending on the day and work schedule). Tim casually straps on the microphone, and begins the demonstration by showing the end product he works toward. Throughout the demo, Tim gives an account of glass making and explains the function and history of the tools used, sprinkled with humor and personal accounts when opportunity arises. The audience carefully watches as Tim works with an associate artist to create incredible one-of-a-kind pieces out of blobs and shards of different stages of molten glass. Once in a while, a piece breaks. Guests are heartbroken, having witnessed its birth; however, Tim has learned that it sometimes happens. "Oh, well," he says, "It gives you respect for the pieces in the showroom."

The showroom displays a portion of WGW's collection, as many works are displayed throughout the homes and businesses from Texas to Europe and Asia. Light fixtures, bowls, platters, vases, glasses, and jewelry are shared. If Tim happens to be in the showroom, he'll take the time to explain the process and details to anyone with questions. WGW also employs other glass artists; their work is displayed as well, from whimsical cat-bellied fishbowls to intricate stained glass panels.

While children are welcome (local schools visit regularly), the staff advises adults to consider their personal day's events before scheduling a trip, as kiddos tired from a day in San Marcos' water may not be happy in a display room of delicate art pieces. Wimberley Glass Works is open Monday through Saturday, 10:00 a.m. to 5:00 p.m., and Sunday noon until 5:00 p.m. Glass blowing demonstrations are given daily except Tuesday, with an hour off for lunch, scheduled according to the day's needs.

TEXAS FUN FACT:

Tim deJong received a grant from the Sam Houston Memorial Museum Complex in Huntsville to build an authentic pioneer glass shop. He is the demonstrating glass blowing artist at the annual Sam Houston Folk Festival. Tim's starburst chandelier is also displayed at the Museum's main entry hall.

ART

Amon Center Museum

3501 Camp Bowie Blvd.

Fort Worth, TX 76107-2695

(817)738-1933

www.cartermuseum.org

Amon Carter was born in a one room log cabin in Crafton, Texas in 1879. His family struggled while growing up, and he was not always afforded the opportunity to enjoy what he later called "advantages". Hard working Carter never gave up. It is said that he even sold peaches from his own farm to support the newspaper he worked for as business manager. Carter eventually became president and publisher of the Fort Worth *Star-Telegram* newspaper in 1923. In 1928, Carter dipped into the oil business, and struck "black gold". The financial success he obtained finally afforded him the opportunity to experience the "advantages" he missed out on in his youth.

Amon Carter had a passion for American art- Western, in particular. Two favorites, whom he collected regularly and extensively, were Frederic Remington and Charles M. Russell. His dream was to display his collections for the public. That dream, and some, would come true, but not within Carter's lifetime. Amon Carter died in 1955. His daughter, Ruth Carter Stevenson, undertook her father's wishes, and the Amon Carter Museum opened its doors to the public in 1961—free of charge(stipulated in his will), so that all could experience the "advantages" of life.

And what advantages they are! The Amon Carter Museum has been expanded twice since the first opening, housing extensive, and quality collections of American art. Collections include paintings, illustrated books, sculptures, photographs and drawings, from well-known artists such as Winslow Homer, Georgia O'Keefe, Frederic Church, Eliot Porter, Alexander Calder, and of course, Frederic Remington and Charles M. Russell.

The museum's permanent collection may be viewed free of charge, but some special events or exhibits may charge to cover the cost of the program. Free tours of the permanent collection are offered Friday through Sunday at 2:00 p.m., starting at the information desk. Photography tours are at 3:00 p.m. on Saturday afternoons. The Museum hosts an enormous number of educational workshops (some have a fee), and select Sundays are free "Family Fundays"—two hours of hands on fun and learning. During extended hours on Thursdays, the special exhibits can be viewed by all at no charge.

The Amon Carter Museum is open 10:00 a.m. to 5:00 p.m., Monday through Wednesday and Friday, 10:00 a.m. until 8:00 p.m. on Thursdays, and noon to 5:00 p.m. on Sundays. They are closed Mondays and major holidays. Parking is available on two lots—Camp Bowie Blvd. (north) and Lancaster Avenue (south). Photography permits are required for personal use photos (no flashes).

The ACM also offers visitors a Cultural District walking tour brochure about the nearby sculptures. It's a great learning tool, used as an individual or with a group. Questions on the guide note common themes with the art pieces, and encourage analysis and comparison thinking. Parents are also offered ideas on how to incorporate art into children's lives, as well as how to prepare children for an art museum visit. These tools are also available on the website. For those interested in Amon Carter's collection of art, but not able to visit the museum, virtual lessons and teaching guides are also available on the website under the "Online Teaching Resources" section.

The Art Center of Corpus Christi

100 Shoreline Drive

Corpus Christi, TX 78401

(361) 884-6406

www.artcentercc.org

Local artists shine at the Art Center of Corpus Christi, where there is always something new. The Center is home to fourteen art groups and 600 unaffiliated individual artists, so it is easy to see why there is a display turnaround often—every month to be exact. Blessed with many artists, the Art Center shares each piece of work proudly within the many rooms of the building. Mediums include oils, acrylics, watercolor, ceramics, metal, fiber, (and more), incorporated into various 2-D and 3-D works of art. Pieces range from intricate pieces of jewelry to wall-sized creations, and everything in between. Realism and surrealism, abstract and concrete—there is something for everyone to enjoy. If not, there's always next month.

Most items on display at the Art Center are for sale; however, there is no pressure to purchase. Art is displayed throughout the building, including the gift shop, on-site restaurant, working studio and even the restrooms! The center staff is welcoming and willing to answer any questions. Outside, the photogenic courtyard faces the gulf, where a never ending coastal breeze makes for an enjoyable time, even in the hottest of weather.

The Art Center of Corpus Christi offers classes to the public, as well as facility rentals. Both services have a cost associated, which is how the ACCC funds free admission to the art galleries. The Art Center of Corpus Christi is open Tuesday through Sunday, 10:00 a.m. to 4:00 p.m. For information about current exhibitions or classes, call or consult the website.

Ellen Noël Art Museum of the Permian Basin

4909 E. University Blvd.

Odessa, TX 79762

(432) 550-9696

http://www.noelartmuseum.org

Opened in 1985 as the Art Institute for the Permian Basin, the Ellen Noël Art Museum of the Permian Basin is a self-proclaimed "Cultural Oasis". The justly nicknamed Museum is accredited by the American Association of Museums and provides residents and visitors with over 20,000 square feet of gallery space. The three galleries house rotating exhibits- either from the museum's permanent collection, or loan exhibits from other art museums. Collections run the gamut of artistic styles- from traditional to contemporary.

The Ellen Noël Art Museum of the Permian Basin also hosts the Arthaus—an educational facility focused on artistic skill and appreciation development for learners of all ages. The Arthaus, in addition to other educational events offer free story times, art activities, games, and programs to the public in exchange for the company and pleasure of guests only. "Brown Bag Educational Series" are a popular lunch time events for college students and professionals, while younger visitors enjoy the hands-on art projects.

The ENAMPB is certainly an extraordinary artistic facility, but they don't stop there. The Museum Foundation is deeply invested in the education and development of those with disabilities. They have created and dedicated a Sculpture and Sensory Garden next to the art museum. In this garden, visitors, regardless of ability level, can experience the plants and sculptures- visually, tactilely, or by scent and sound. All sculptures are hands-on, able to be touched and interpreted, or in some instances, played. Braille and audio tours are available, as well as sight assisted tours for the blind. For visitors interested in experiencing the garden with a sensory disability, the museum staff also provides disability awareness training, using a blindness simulator. The garden has played an invaluable part in the raised student, teacher, and medical staff awareness for those with disabilities in the West Texas area. The Arthaus welcomes students with disabilities as well, often including lesson and activities that involve multiple senses. Check the website or call for a schedule of current activities.

The Ellen Noël Art Museum of the Permian Basin is located on the University of Texas of the Permian Basin campus. It is open Tuesday through Saturday, 10:00 a.m. to 5:00 p.m. and Sundays 2:00 p.m. until 5:00 p.m.

TEXAS FUN FACT:

Texas is the only state to enter the United States by treaty instead of territorial annexation.

El Paso Museum of Art

One Arts Festival Plaza

El Paso, TX 79901

(915) 532-1707

www.elpasoartmuseum.org

The El Paso Museum of Art found its beginnings in 1925 as the brainchild of Kate Moore Brown, president of the women's department of the El Paso Chamber of Commerce. After some legwork, a charter for the El Paso International Museum was granted in 1930, but the collection was growing, and there was no building to display the items. In the 1940's, Mrs. Iva Turney deeded her and her late husband William's 1910 Neoclassical Revival home to the museum board, and the collection was open for viewing in 1947. In 1959, the name changed to El Paso Museum of Art after additions to the building and the deed was transferred to the City of El Paso. It was renovated again in 1960; necessity mandated the growth to encompass the newly acquired Samuel H. Kress Collection-three galleries worth of paintings and sculptures.

Today, visitors can still enjoy the three galleries of the Kress Collection. The works include artists from the 13th-18th centuries, divided into the galleries visually by wall partitions and colors. Ornate frames trim works by artists Jusepe de Ribera, Giovanni di Paolo, Bernardo Strozzi, Anthony van Dyck and others.

Although the Renaissance and Baroque pieces are definitely worth the trip, visitors find the Contemporary works quite enjoyable as well. Spotlighted are Luis Jimenez, Gaspar Enriquez, Jose Cisneros, Manuel Acosta and Tom Lea—all "Sons of El Paso". Tom Lea has an entire gallery dedicated to his striking paintings of the southwest and her people. The museum is also host to a number of visiting collections, with an emphasis on area life—past and present.

The El Paso Museum of Art is open Tuesday, Wednesday, Friday and Saturday from 9:00 a.m. to 5:00 p.m. Thursday's hours are 9:00 a.m. to

9:00 p.m., and Sundays noon to 5:00 p.m. They are closed Mondays and major holidays. Free docent led tours are offered daily, in English and Spanish, and usually last about 45 minutes. The museum auditorium occasionally shows free foreign films; check the website or call for details.

TEXAS FUN FACT:

Texas has more than 100 post office murals painted by local artists during the Great Depression. The paintings were commissioned to provide hope and a sense of community during this time of hardship in our history.

TEXAS FUN FACT:

Texas serves as the habitat for the nation's largest herd of whitetail deer.

First State Bank of Uvalde

200 East Nopal

Uvalde, TX 78801

(830) 278-6231

www.fsbuvalde.com

Stopping in Uvalde is intriguing. Ask any of the residents for town interest spots, and chances are, the First State Bank of Uvalde will come up in the conversation. At first, it may seem odd for the entire town to boast, "You just HAVE to see the bank!" However, once visitors step through the doors, a wave of understanding overcomes any initial apprehension of going on a sightseeing tour of "the town bank."

The bank's history is interesting enough, boasting leader involvement of John Nance Garner (32nd vice president of the United States) and Dolph Briscoe Jr. (former Governor of Texas). Started in 1907, the institution has survived a few building moves, the Depression, and a mandatory ten-day closing declared by Governor "Ma" Ferguson—impressive feats of the time, but certainly nothing to make the bank necessarily a tourist stop when traveling through southwest Texas.

So what is it that makes the stop worthwhile? Janey Briscoe's vision and initiative. Before her husband served as Governor of Texas in the 70's, the First State Bank of Uvalde grew into the current 1969 building. Janey saw it as her mission to be the official bank decorator. However, traditional bank décor was not her vision; she strove to instill a sense of family within the bank's walls by choosing draperies, flooring, furniture and art pieces as if she were designing her own home. The facility warmed up as she filled it with antiques and art—all with a western flair.

Today, bank employees welcome visitors—bank patrons and out-of-towners alike—to come view the pieces chosen by and in memory of Janey Briscoe. Paintings adorn the walls, numerous yet elegant, including a portrait of the bank's First Lady (oh, and Governor Briscoe is beside her). Bronze sculptures and animal mounts, antique Oriental rugs and jewel toned leather seating all provide that "welcome home" feel that was Janey's focus. Available personnel are happy to show off the collection, and even share piece-specific stories as time allows. From single family tours to busloads, First Uvalde Bank is a stop visitors will not soon forget.

The First State Bank of Uvalde lobby is open 9:00 a.m. until 3:00 p.m., Monday through Friday. Visitors wishing to view the "museum" are welcome at any time, but call first for large groups or to ensure a guide.

TEXAS FUN FACT:

There is more land used as farmland in Texas than in any other state.

TEXAS FUN FACT:

Onions are the leading vegetable crop in Texas—so much that the state vegetable is the "1015 Sweet Onion," named for its traditional October 15 planting date.

Kimbell Art Museum

3333 Camp Bowie Blvd.

Fort Worth, TX 76107-2792

(817) 332-8451

www.kimbellart.org

The Kimbell Art Museum opened in 1966 as a tribute to Kay Kendall, a successful miller and industrialist of the Fort Worth area. Starting with Kendall's personal collection, his wife, Velma, carried out his wishes after his death in 1964 by dedicating their entire estate to the development of the museum. Their vision was a small collection of the highest standards, to highlight and appreciate aesthetics of each significant work of art.

Louis I. Khan designed the building that houses the Kimbell collection, and is indeed a piece of art itself. Natural light reflected by metal illuminates the cylindrical architecture and the treasures within—Cezanne, Matisse, Rembrandt, Fra Angelico—paintings and sculptures range from worldwide antiquities to 20th century artists. The presentation of the artwork is immaculate; the crispness of line centers visitors' eyes on the masterpieces, ready for a look into the artist's eye. Courtyards and a reflecting pool on the grounds complete this modern-day work of art.

Although Kimbell Art Museum's focus is on high-quality masterpieces that epitomize era and style, they are quite family friendly. Family Festivals are on select Saturdays from 1:00 p.m. to 4:00 p.m., and feature hands-on art activities, film programs, storytelling, and personal connections with the gallery's masterpieces. The KAM's information desk also offers a family gallery guide focusing on pieces of their permanent collection, with picture cards, fun facts, and discussion questions. For those interested in more in-depth information about the art, free lectures are offered on Friday nights and Saturdays; see the website or call for specific covered topics.

The Kimbell Art Museum is open Tuesday through Thursday, 10:00 a.m. to 5:00 p.m., Friday noon until 8:00 p.m., Saturday 10:00 a.m. to

5:00 p.m., and Sunday noon to 5:00 p.m. They are closed Mondays, New Year's Day, 4th of July, Thanksgiving, and Christmas Day. Special exhibits may have a charge, but for the permanent collection, tours (Wednesday at 2:00 p.m. and Sunday at 3:00 p.m.) and viewing are always free. Free parking is available off of Arch Adams and Darnell Streets.

TEXAS FUN FACT:

The world famous Fort Worth Livestock Exchange was commonly featured in the hit 1980's drama *Dallas*.

Lillie and Hugh Roy Cullen Sculpture Garden

1001 Bissonnet

Houston, TX 77265-6826

(713) 639-7300

www.mfah.org/sculpturegarden

The Lillie and Hugh Roy Cullen Sculpture Garden is a virtual unknown cubby of beauty in Houston's Museum District. Designed by world-renown Isamu Noguchi, the garden opened in 1986, encompassed by walls ranging from eight to fourteen feet. The Museum of Fine Arts opposed the walls at Noguchi's first proposal, saying that the inclusive atmosphere created an "elitist" feel, whereas they wanted to make the garden welcoming and accessible to all visitors. However, Noguchi insisted that the partitions provided a noise barrier and helped create a sense of place, and was integral to his design. The Museum agreed to let Noguchi follow through with his plan, and time has proven both entities right in their thinking.

On a corner between the Museum of Fine Arts and the Contemporary Arts Museum, the Sculpture Garden is easy to miss, despite the multiple entrances. Two entrances face the parking lot across from the Museum of Fine Arts, and one is off the sidewalk on Montrose. Once inside, though, visitors find that the reduced noise coupled with the varying metal structures makes for a peaceful time spent alone or with others, admiring the art.

The Cullen Sculpture Garden holds twenty five works from the Museum of Fine Arts collection, along with other pieces on loan. Works include examples of Modernism, Post Modernism, Surrealism, Biomorphic Abstraction, and Abstract Construction. Artists include Henri Matisse, Alexander Calder, David Smith, Joan Miro', Bryan Hunt, and Louis Bourgeois. The sculptures and surrounding garden (a work of landscaping art itself) is a popular photography spot.

The Cullen Sculpture Garden is open 9:00 a.m. to 10:00 p.m. daily. Various museums are nearby, such as the Museum of Fine Arts Houston, which is free on Thursdays, and the Contemporary Arts Museum. Next door to the CAM, the Jung Center offers free admission to the student art gallery. For visitors with children, The Children's Museum of Houston is also nearby on Binz (about 5 blocks away), and has Free Family Nights on Thursdays between 5:00 p.m. until 8:00 p.m. The Health Museum also offers Free Family Thursdays from 2:00 p.m. to 5:00 p.m. Check out www.houstonmuseumdistrict.org for details and maps to these and other area museums when planning a Houston trip.

TEXAS FUN FACT:

The Astrodome was built in 1965 by Judge Roy Hofheinz, then owner of the Houston Astros baseball team. It is the first domed stadium built in the United States, and was known for many years as Hofheinz proclaimed it: The Eighth Wonder of the World.

Menil Collection

1515 Sul Rose

Houston, TX 77006

(713) 525-9400

www.menil.org

At home in the Museum District of Houston, the Menil Collection was the vision and gift of John and Dominique de Menil in 1987 after John's death in 1973. With additions to their private contribution, the Menil Collection now has more than 16,000 pieces of art shared either through the primary facility or on loan to other museums. Special traveling exhibits are also shown at the Menil.

John and Dominique de Menil came to the oil business in America from France during World War II. The couple thrived in John's new business position, CEO of Schulumberger, Ltd. (owned by Dominique's father), and quickly became well-known figures in the Houston area. As their popularity grew so did their collections. John and Dominique de Menil did not only collect art, however, they befriended many of the artists and encouraged appreciation and expression through artistic venues throughout their lives. Friends of the de Menils shown in the museum include: Max Ernst, Rene' Magritte, Robert Rauschenberg, Mark Rothko, and Andy Warhol.

The building that houses the art is a piece of work itself. Spanning numerous blocks in the mixed residential/business neighborhood, the museum is a collection of large spaces and cubbyholes. Skylights and large windows provide natural light most of the time, the labels are simple, and there are no audio tours, encouraging personal interpretation. Inside, visitors find the treasures of Picasso, Ray, and Matisse alongside the nameless artists of centuries past.

The African sculptures are found in a virtual jungle—glass walls protect the art from weather while allowing in the beauty of the surrounding arboretum. The Surrealism display is cozy, encouraging personal interactions with the art (no touching, of course!) An interesting section to view is the "Witnesses to a Surrealist Vision", a collection of objects owned by Surrealist artists. An informational brochure is available outside of the room to explain the purpose and importance of these pieces.

The Menil Collection is quite eclectic; such a gathering of ancient objects and contemporary pieces together is a rare sight. The Menil Foundation continues the philanthropic ideals of John and Dominique—art is to be shared—so the museum is free and open to visitors Wednesdays through Sundays, 11:00 a.m. until 7:00 p.m. Free parking is also available a block over at 1515 West Alabama.

Within walking distance of the main building are other attractions related to the Menil Collection. Rothko Chapel (10:00 a.m. to 6:00 p.m.) was commissioned by the de Menils in 1971. It highlights fourteen of Rothko's abstract art pieces for reflection and contemplation. The Dan Flavin Instillation at Richmond Hall (Wednesday-Sunday, 11:00 a.m. until 7:00 p.m.) "highlights" the Minimalist through his interpretation of light as an art medium in the 1930 Weingarten's Grocery building. The exhibit is Flavin's last work before he died in 1996, and Dominique de Menil's final commission before she passed away the next year.

The Byzantine Fresco Chapel Museum safeguards thirteenth century frescoes from Cyprus. The frescoes were removed from their original site, and cut into 38 pieces when the Menil Foundation paid the ransom and returned the pieces to the Church of Cyprus. The Foundation now has two pieces in the Chapel Museum displayed in elegant surroundings of frosted glass and metal, highlighting the detail through simplicity.

The Old Jail Art Center

201 South Second Street

Albany, TX 76430

(325) 762-2269

www.theoldjailartcenter.org

The Old Jail Art Center opened its doors in 1980, over 100 years after the building's construction as Shackelford County's first jail in 1878. The building was completed by Scottish stonemasons (look for their initials on the outside stones) at a cost of $9000. In 1940, the county moved to a larger facility, and the Old Jail was bought for a mere $25 by Robert E. Nail, local author and playwright. Upon his passing, his nephew, Reilly inherited the structure. Reilly and his cousin Bill Bomar opened the Old Jail Art Center with their family collections.

The OJAC now has over 1900 pieces to share, varying from Eastern (Chinese Terra-Cotta tomb figures) to Western (Lambshead Ranch collection of functional art and artifacts), and everything in between. The OJAC has pieces from French artists, including Renoir and Toulouse-Lautrec, and pre-Columbian art vessels, as well as a number of large outdoor sculptures displayed in the Marshall R. Young Courtyard. They even possess a Picasso and Miro. The big artist names draw interest to the museum, but the stories, collection and charm of the building and staff are what make a trip to the Old Jail Art Center enjoyable.

The Old Jail Art Center is open Tuesday through Saturday from 10:00 a.m. until 5:00 p.m., and Sunday from 2:00 p.m. until 5:00 p.m. They are closed Mondays and most holidays. The building is on the National Register of Historic Places, as is the Shackelford County courthouse District located at 225 South Main in Albany.

TEXAS FUN FACT:

Robert E. Nail is most known for his play, *The Fort Griffin Fandangle*. Albany continues to produce the 1938 pioneer musical every June. See www.albanytexas.com for details.

Stark Museum of Art

712 Green Ave.

Orange, TX 77630

(409) 883-6661

www.starkmuseum.org

Orange-born H.J. Lutcher Stark and his (third) wife, Nelda, together developed the Stark Foundation in 1961—sharing their artistic vision with the community. Before his death in 1965, Lutcher created the Shangri-La Botanical Gardens, and after Nelda took over as chairperson, the Stark Museum of Art opened in 1978, and plans were rolling for the Lutcher Theatre, renovation of the Stark House and Stark Park. Nelda oversaw these and other projects of the Stark Foundation until her death in 1999.

The lobby of the Stark Museum of Art warmly invites visitors with Native American blanket-lined walls surrounding Buck McCain's sculpture, "The Invocation". Two stories of collections include paintings, porcelain works, bronze statues and functional Native American items, with a primary focus on pieces from the 1820's until present time. The SMA features many artists, including Robert Henri, Alexander Hogue, William Herbert Dunton, and a large collection from naturalist John James Audubon. There is a charming assortment of Southwestern and natural art pieces to enjoy, as these types were personal favorites of the Starks. Crystal enthusiasts may enjoy the museum's set of "The United States in Crystal"—the only known complete set of engraved bowls by Steuben Glass.

The Stark Museum of Art is open from 10:00 a.m. until 5:00 p.m. Tuesday through Saturday. It is closed Sunday, Monday, New Year's Day, Easter, 4th of July, thanksgiving and Christmas Day. Programs, presentations and tours are provided free of charge, but please call for information about subjects or to set up a guided tour.

BEER AND WINE

Cap*Rock Winery

408 E. Woodrow Rd.

Lubbock, TX 79423

(806) 863-2704

www.caprockwinery.com

Cap*Rock winery began in 1992 under the current owners, the Plains National Corporation. Named for the summit of a mesa, the winery is the third largest in Texas. They currently use grapes from local growers, but developing plans for a vineyard should come to "fruition" by 2011.

A visit to Cap*Rock will take parties through the winemaking process. Tours take place every half-hour during the business day and workers show the future vineyard, gathering equipment, processing machines, barrels, casks and bottling lines. Cap*Rock's building is 23,000 square feet—with the capacity to produce 45,000 cases and house 90,000 cases of wine. The building is an elegantly decorated Southwestern Mission style structure with various art and sculpture pieces throughout. Guests enjoy the warm atmosphere of the tasting room while sipping complimentary tastes of the full spectrum of wines that Cap*Rock offers.

Cap*Rock Winery is open Monday through Saturday, 10:00 a.m. until 5:00 p.m., and Sunday noon-5:00 p.m. If interested, the stylish rooms in the winery are available for rent; see the website for details.

TEXAS FUN FACT:

No part of the grape is wasted during the winemaking process. Stems are used as ingredients in facial creams, seeds are used for grape seed oil, and the skins and leftover pulp are recycled as fertilizer for new plants in the vineyards.

Llano Estacado Winery

PO Box 3487

Lubbock, TX 79452

(800) 634-3854

www.llanowine.com

Llano Estacado began in 1976 under the direction of three Texas Tech professors, releasing 1,300 cases in 1977. The small winery had many surprises ahead. By 1980, Llano Estacado planted its own grapes and the quickly increasing production numbers led to the 1983 equipment upgrade. In 1986, the winery's 1984 Chardonnay surprisingly won Double Gold in the San Francisco Fair Wine Competition, and the awards have not stopped since. Today, Llano Estacado produces upwards around 120,000 cases of award-winning wines per year.

Tasting room visitors will find eager, friendly guides sharing knowledge of the winemaking process and history of the company. Workers share every bit of the grapes' progression, from vine to wine. Unusual, though integral, the tour starts with information about barrel and cork making, explaining the differences and importance of each. Though the process is similar regardless of the winery visiting, the Llano Estacado staff delightfully explain details and point out subtle differences between their choices and typical winemaking. Visitors are able to see storage and bottling equipment; lucky ones may see the process in action (depending on season).

After the tour, complimentary tastings are available in a variety of preferences—from fruity whites to spicy reds, not to mention, a lovely choice of ports. Tasting wines are available for purchase in the store, along with gift baskets and other wine paraphernalia (shipping information is available in the store as well as online). Tours are available every half-hour, Monday through Saturday, 10:00 a.m. to 5:00 p.m., and Sunday noon to 5:00 p.m.

Piney Woods Country Wines

3408 Willow Drive

Orange, TX 77632

(888) 857-9575

www.pineywoodswines.com

Alfred Flies, the 80-something-year-old East Texan remembers his dad's homemade wine, created from the backyard plum tree. This childhood memory of Prohibition grew his interest and now it is he that makes the wine. In 1987, Alfred's public doors opened, ready to share his family tradition with visitors from all over the world.

Historically, the term "country wine" refers to beverages made from fermented fruits. Grapes are not necessarily included, although muscadine grapes are, as they are native to the area. Since the winemaking depends on available fruits, the winery's vintage may vary drastically from season to season. Piney Woods Country Wines has processed blackberry, peach, plum, orange, muscadine, and pear, but their most popular is the blueberry wine (Perhaps, due to the numerous blueberry farms nearby!)

There is a range of tastes to meet everyone's palette, from dry to sweet, but the majority of Alfred's nectar comes out sweet and fruity- what else? Customers rave for the versatility; wine can be enjoyed as is, mixed with sauces, or even poured over ice cream. Like a taste? Stop by any day but Sunday. Piney Woods Country Wines is open from 9:00 a.m. until 5:00 p.m., and the property is open for self guided tours. Give them a call if a guided tour is more your speed—he'll be happy to show you around and share his story.

Sister Creek Vineyards

1142 Sisterdale Road

Sisterdale, TX 78006

(830) 324-6704

www.sistercreekvineyards.com

The Sisterdale settlement began in 1845 under the leadership of Nicolas Zink, a German surveyor of New Braunfels. Located between the East and West Sister Creeks on present-day FM 1376, early settlers soon decided that Sisterdale did not fit their lifestyle preferences—poets and writers do not a farm make. By 1850 the area transformed into a hydropathic institute, *Badenthal*, an effort to encourage well-being through mineral water therapy, founded by Ernst Kapp and Dr. Rudolph Wipprecht.

1885 brought a cotton gin to the community of Sisterdale, although it closed in 1927, due to the local boll-weevil infestation that shut the area's investment in cotton down completely. Today, the gin building still stands. Restored, it contains the Sister Creek winery.

Sister Creek Vineyards was established in 1988. The winery provides self-guided tour sheets, and allows guests to leisurely browse the winery and grounds, asking questions of the employees as need arises. The guides are informative, and when finished, winery guests are welcome to a complimentary taste of three Sister Creek wine styles.

Sister Creek Vineyards is a down-home, friendly establishment. They welcome families and leashed pets (but only serve to adults). The Vineyard is located between Boerne and Fredericksburg—two popular shopping/golf areas in the Texas Hill Country. The Vineyard tasting room is open Monday through Friday, 10:00 a.m. to 5:00 p.m., Saturday 10:00 a.m. to 5:30 p.m., and Sunday noon until 5:30 p.m.

Spoetzl Brewery

603 Brewery

Shiner, TX 77984

(361) 594-3383

www.shiner.com

When the name "Shiner" is spoken most Texans think of beer—and rightfully so, as Shiner is home to the Spoetzl Brewery, the oldest independent brewery in Texas.

In 1909, the Czech and German immigrants of "Blue Moon" (previous name for the town of Shiner) longed for the old-world brews left behind in Europe. They began brewing small batches of beer, named themselves Shiner Brewing Association, and the rest, as is said, is history.

In 1913, the men hired Bavarian Kosmos Spoetzl as brewmaster. He improved on the recipe, upgraded the brewery, and then bought the company outright in 1915. His handcrafted beer gained popularity in the German-Czech community. During Prohibition (1920-1933), Spoetzl Brewery survived throughout by making and distributing ice and birch beer, but some say Kosmos continued beer brewing for his friends and the area farmers.

1947 brought a facelift to the Shiner brewery when Spoetzl had the building refaced with white brick; the same look and old-world feel is around today. After Kosmos died in 1950, the brewery was renamed K. Spoetzl Brewery in his honor.

During the 1960's and 1970's, the brewery had less than 1% of the Texas beer market. After changing hands again in 1989, the brewery increased production and started distributing to other states besides Texas. They experienced much success; so much that the brewery dedicated $40 million to expand itself in 1995. Though the equipment is now bigger and better than ever, it is the continued handcrafting that makes the beer truly special.

Brewery tours are given Monday through Friday, 11:00 a.m. and 1:30 p.m. On the tour, visitors will learn about the history of the brewery as well as the brewing process, packaging, and distribution. The tour ends in the hospitality room where guests can enjoy a generous taste of exactly what has made Shiner famous.

TEXAS FUN FACT:

Although they are not big fans of beer, turkeys are a common site at wine vineyards due to the fact that they love grapes!

Texas Hills Vineyards

P.O. Box 1480

Johnson City, TX 78636

(830) 868-2321

http://www.texashillsvineyard.com

Welcome to the home of the first Pinot Grigio wine in Texas! Texas Hills Vineyards is off of 290 on Ranch Road 2766 in Johnson City, a few miles from the Pedernales River State Park. Speckled with vineyards, the Texas Hill Country boasts soil similar to that in the Tuscan Valley in Italy. However, Texas Hills Vineyard goes beyond others by offering free tastings and tours of the winery. "Wines to share with friends" is the motto, and friendly faces share the story of the company from its beginnings in 1999.

Texas Hills Vineyard uses organic and environmentally sound methods throughout the growth of their facilities. Not only are the grapes organically grown, but the winery and tasting room is built up from the very earth that surrounds it (formally known as "rammed earth"). The building sports no windows in attempts to keep the temperature consistent to properly develop the wine (it also provides a nice environment for the visitors!).

The owners welcome visitors to drop by the tasting room or patio during business hours; they also participate in various wine and social area events. The room is open Monday through Saturday, 10:00 a.m. until 5:00 p.m., and Sunday noon to 5:00 p.m.

Val Verde Winery

100 Qualia Dr.

Del Rio, TX 78840

(830) 775-9714

www.valverdewinery.com

A few miles from the Mexican border, visitors to Del Rio can find the oldest continuously running winery in Texas- Val Verde Winery. Established in 1883 by Italian immigrant Frank Qualia, the winery is now run by the Qualia's great-grandson, Thomas. The four-generation, single family ownership of the land and business has earned this vineyard the Land Heritage Award recognition from the Department of Agriculture.

Thomas is dedicated to the traditions and expertise handed down to him, and takes great care in creating the Val Verde Wines. The Winery carries a selection of whites, reds, and Thomas' award-winning Don Lois Tawny Port. Visitors are welcome to stop by for complimentary tours and tastings (Must be 21 to drink!), but if a specific wine is wanted, please call ahead for availability. During the tour, visitors will enjoy the story of Val Verde's beginnings, as well as a description of the wine making process. The Winery is open from 10:00 a.m. until 5:00 p.m. Monday through Saturday.

Val Verde Winery is located in the Historic Del Rio residential neighborhood. Look for the inviting, vine-covered street side sign, and happy faces, welcoming visitors to share in the family pride.

FARMS AND GARDENS

Amarillo Zoo in Thompson Park

Thompson Park (NE 24th and Fillmore)

Amarillo, TX 79107

(806) 381-7911

www.amarilloparks.org

Looking to provide leisure opportunities throughout Amarillo for citizens and visitors, the city's Parks and Recreation Department currently manages over 60 parks around the city. Included is Thompson Memorial Park, home to the Amarillo Zoo. While this facility is not as large as other ticketed zoological gardens throughout the state, it is worth the stopover while in the Panhandle.

Immediately through the front gate of the zoo, guests giggle at the antics of the community of spider monkeys while they climb trees, built shelters, and each other. Other animals in the park include black bears, African lions, a Bengal tiger, and Bennett's wallabies, as well as regional animals such as bobcats, grey foxes, coyotes, mustangs, and bison. The zoo's new herpetarium brings more species to observe.

The Amarillo Zoo does not have printed maps; however, each exhibit has labels and informational signs appropriate to the site. After visiting, *paletta* (Mexican popsicle) vendors are usually accessible, especially in hotter months. The zoo is open Tuesday through Sunday, 9:30 a.m. to 5:30 p.m.

Thompson Memorial Park has a number of picnicking areas, playgrounds, athletic courts and a disk golf course. During the summer, the Thompson Park Pool is open, but there is a small pool fee to swim.

Chihuahuan Desert Gardens at the University of Texas El Paso

Corner of University and Wiggens- UTEP Campus

El Paso, TX 79968

(915) 747-5565

http://museum.utep.edu

Desert Gardens? To the untrained botanist, this may seem like an oxymoron; however the University of Texas at El Paso has taken the challenge of training plant enthusiasts of all ages and interests. The Chihuahuan Desert Garden at UTEP is a literal oasis in the desert. The fifteen-section garden houses more than 625 different species of native plants, from the thriving Mexican Hats (Ratibida columnifera) to the endangered Organ Mountains Evening Primrose (Oenothera organensis). The UTEP staff offer maps and self-guided walking tour information of the garden (3 pages for those with average interest and 5 pages for the avid gardener). The printable general tour is also available in Spanish. Visitors can peruse through the agaves, yucca plants, Texas mountain laurel, desert marigolds, beargrass, Texas persimmons, and many others—as the season allows. Other interesting features include a delicate dripping bell fountain and a prayer wheel given to the garden in 2003 by the people of Bhutan.

The Chihuahuan Desert Gardens have multiple goals. In addition to providing a relaxing atmosphere for people to enjoy, the university uses the gardens as a formal and informal teaching tool. Landscaping and water conservation techniques are demonstrated throughout the garden and explained upon request. Vital information about the Chihuahuan Desert's vegetative inhabitants for botany students (or enthusiasts) is also shared. The online site provides the mentioned tour guides, as well as an extensive database of plants featured in the garden and others native to the Chihuahuan Desert.

The online site provides a wealth of information for research before and during a trip. Activity ideas and directions, plant and animal checklists, informational publications, virtual exhibits, online courses, regional information and much more will inform and interest even those whose thumbs are not-so-green in preparation for a visit.

As if the Desert Garden were not enough, within the garden grounds is UTEP's Centennial Museum. The museum provides informational exhibits about the natural and cultural history of the Chihuahuan Desert region. The museum hosts free educational events throughout the school year, often coinciding with garden events and features. Admission to the Centennial Museum is also free.

The Chihuahuan Desert Garden is open daily from dawn until dusk. The Centennial Museum is open Tuesday through Saturday from 10:00 a.m. until 4:30 p.m. They are both closed on university holidays.

TEXAS FUN FACT:

The 1857 Engine No. 1 was recently restored and moved to a new location at Union Plaza. Virtual Exhibit "The Restoration of Engine No. 1" takes web visitors through the process from the engine's 42 year stay at UTEP to its new home.

Houston Arboretum and Nature Center

4501 Woodway Dr.

Houston, TX 77024-7708

(866) 510-7219

www.houstonarboretum.org

On the grounds of Camp Logan, a World War I Army training camp, now stands one of Houston's most incredible attractions—the Houston Arboretum and Nature Center. Houston's Memorial Park was dedicated in 1924 to the fallen soldiers of the Great War, and in 1951, a section of the park was set aside as a nature preserve. That preserve, the Houston Arboretum, along with the 1967 Nature Center now coexist with the same goal: to protect nature through education.

A trip to the Houston Arboretum Visitor Center will provide tourists with extensive information about the animals and plants in the arboretum. Trail maps, checklists, and information booklets are readily available to take on hikes on over 5 miles of trails in the 155 acre sanctuary. While on the trails, hikers have the opportunity to see Texan native plant and animal life, such as Texas Mountain Laurel and Yaupon Holly, or Gulf Coast Toads, Pileated Woodpeckers, and maybe even a Nine-Banded Armadillo (given the proper time of day, naturally).

The Nature Center's Discovery Room provides interactive exhibits for children, explaining what may not easily be seen to an untrained eye. Microscopes, discovery boxes and games help facilitate learning through the guise of "having fun". The room is popular with area schools; if planning a visit during March, April, or May, visitors may want to phone ahead to check for scheduled guests.

The Houston Arboretum also offers educational programs to nature enthusiasts—the Urban Nature Series, offered on the second and fourth Sundays of each month, is a free class for families and/or individuals. Other feed classes are also available. Check the website or call for presentation details.

The grounds and trails are open daily 7:00 a.m. until 7:00 p.m. Guided tours are offered free of charge at 2:00 p.m. and 3:00 p.m. on Saturdays. The Discovery Room is open Tuesday through Sunday, 10:00 a.m. until 4:00 p.m. and offers Nature Story Time on the first Sunday of each month. The Nature Center Building is open 9:00 a.m. to 5:00 p.m. daily.

TEXAS FUN FACT:

The Port of Houston is the 10th largest port in the world, and it is also ranks as the top port in the United States in international commerce.

Japanese "Sunken" Tea Garden

3853 N. St. Mary's St.

San Antonio, TX 78212

(210) 735-0663

www.sanantonio.gov/sapar/japanhis.asp

Located near the San Antonio Zoo in Brackenridge Park, the Japanese Tea Gardens is a virtual paradise. Visitors step into another world—one of serene pools, delicate pebble walkways, arched bridges, a 60-foot waterfall, and a Japanese pagoda, filled with flourishing and colorful plant life. Nature and Man's artistic vision provide a peaceful backdrop to various photographic opportunities or even a simple walk to enjoy the beauty.

Hard to believe, the Sunken Gardens' beginnings come from a limestone quarry in the early 1900's. The quarry was closed in 1908 and the land beside it was donated to the City of San Antonio by Mrs. Emma Koehler (widow of Pearl Brewery's Otto Koehler) for use as a city park in 1915. The City Parks Commissioner spent $7000 and numerous hours of prison labor to develop his vision for a section of the park—the Japanese Gardens—by 1919. The actual quarry is now the Japanese Sunken Garden Theater; the amphitheater regularly hosts commercial and city sponsored events.

Kimi Eizo Jingu, a San Antonio Japanese-American artist, was commissioned in 1926 to further develop the garden, and his family continued to work there until 1942 after Mr. Jingu's death in 1930. At this point, due to World War II, community citizens were outraged with the Japanese, and the Jingu family was evicted. The garden was renamed as "Chinese", but in 1984, the area was once again dedicated as the Japanese Sunken Gardens.

The Japanese Sunken Gardens are open daily from 5:00 a.m. until dark.

Lyndon B. Johnson State Park and Historic Site:
Sauer-Beckmann Living History Farmstead

P.O. Box 238

Stonewall, TX 78671

(830) 644-2252

http://communication.utexas.edu/sauerbeckmann

Visitors take a step back in time to German Texan farm life circa 1915-1918. Historical interpreters, in period dress, perform daily chores while sharing stories about the history of the farmstead with visitors. It is not unusual for visitors to help carry out the tasks of daily life. Feeding and caring for the animals might include milking cows, slopping pigs, collecting eggs, and tending to sheep. The noon meal is cooked on the wood burning stove with an aroma that floats memories to a simpler, more routine era, using only what is grown or raised on the property. Provisions are made for the winter by canning extra fruits and vegetables from the garden, as well as preparing pork sausage in the smokehouse. The restored houses, scrubbed clean with homemade lye soap, share the history (and the flavor!) of the families who previously owned the farm.

Visitors to the farm will find the interpreters quite knowledgeable and pleasant as they share their way of life—far removed from many current-day experiences as there is no electricity or running water in the houses. The farmstead is part of the LBJ State Park; day use picnic areas, hiking trails, and sports facilities are also available for use. The Sauer-Beckmann Living History Farm is open for visitors from 8:00 a.m. until 4:30 p.m. daily, except Thanksgiving Day, Christmas Day and New Year's Day, while the park buildings stay open until 5:00 p.m. Teaching materials for use in conjunction with the farm visit are available on the website.

Mercer Arboretum and Botanic Gardens

22306 Aldine Westfield Road

Humble, TX 77338-1071

(281) 443-8731

www.hcp4.net/mercer

Mercer Arboretum transitions visitors between the Gulf Coast and Piney Woods regions of Texas. Named for the original owners, Thelma and Charles Mercer, the gardens fulfill their dream of sharing the beauty of plants with the community. "Connecting people with plants" is Mercer's motto, clearly upheld through numerous educational activities and informational items in place for visitors.

Mercer Arboretum and Botanical Gardens encompasses more than 250 acres and is the region's largest collection of native and cultivated plants. Twenty seven different themed gardens and attractions are noted on the available maps and plants throughout the gardens are clearly labeled with both scientific and common names. Garden choices include fragrant Herb, Daylily, Vine, Perennial (complete with butterflies and hummingbirds), Tropical, and one of the largest ginger collections in the nation (150 different species). The Prehistoric Garden shares the evolution of plants, while the Endangered Species Garden shows Mercer's efforts to preserve the precious life forms. A must-see for visitors is the Lily Pond and Iris Garden. Nearby is the Bamboo Garden, containing thirty species, some of which tower above in great gatherings.

The west side of the park contains an outdoor classroom, picnic areas, a barbeque pavilion (available to rent) and three miles of walking trails. During garden walks, visitors can enjoy a number of scarecrows, humorous in design as well as name (ex: Elvis Parsley and the Headless Hortman). American Industrial Folk Artist, Andre' Gandin, has whimsical scrap metal sculptures on display throughout the gardens as well.

Mercer Arboretum and Botanical Gardens is an ideal place for photographers. The Arboretum does ask that anyone taking photos to please register in the office and follow the given guidelines. Visiting the MABG is largely a self-guided experience; maps and information are available in the Visitor Center. Group tours are available, but need to be arranged at least three weeks in advance. Summer hours are Monday through Saturday, 8:00 a.m. until 7:00 p.m. and Sunday, 10:00 a.m. until 7:00 p.m. Winter hours are 8:00 a.m. to 5:00 p.m. daily.

TEXAS FUN FACT:

According to local lore, famous billionaire Howard Hughes was born in Humble, TX on Christmas Eve 1905.

Sea Center Texas

300 Medical Drive

Lake Jackson, TX 77566

(979) 292-0100

www.tpwd.state.tx.us/spdest/visitorcenters/seacenter

Sea Center Texas is an establishment of Texas Parks and Wildlife mainly used to promote education and awareness. The facility includes multiple themed aquariums, touch tanks, a wetlands exhibit and a hatchery building. Downloadable teacher (or parent) resources are available on the website for pre-visit activity ideas and are also available as hard copies at the center. The scavenger hunts, checklists, and activity booklets are designed to help focus learning while at the center.

First entry into the visitor center wows guests with over 20 fiberglass reproductions of state record fish, including flounder, blue marlin, and even various sharks. The Nature Center is primarily a self-guided visit, as each area is clearly marked with signs and explanations, or staffed with volunteers, eager to answer any questions that may arise. The children's favorite Touch Tank exhibit allows gentle exploration of hermit crabs, blue crabs, Lightening Whelk, and anemone.

Tourists now proceed to a number of aquariums, each with a specific habitat and group of fish species. Salt Marsh, Coastal Bay, Jetty, Reef, and Gulf of Mexico share the underwater wonder of native Texas habitats, while the Tropical aquarium houses fish found in the Pacific Ocean.

Outside, the Wetlands exhibit gives opportunity to observe birds, other animals and plant life by way of a 600 foot-long boardwalk. Nature checklists and activity booklets are available specifically designed for the wetlands area. Guided tours can be arranged through the Visitor Center free of charge.

The Hatchery Program Building is also available for touring, but it is by guide only. Reservations must be made prior to tour time, and it is advised to call in advance (the free tour has limited visiting times as well as space). In the Hatchery Building, visitors can learn about the TP&WD stock enhancement program. This program helps keep acceptable harvest levels of Red Drum and Spotted Sea Trout by supplementing the natural coastal populations of these fish. The tours last about 45 minutes, and show how the center supports the Sport Fish Restoration Act, by cultivating eggs into "fingerlings" ready for release into the wild.

Sea Center Texas offers a number of educational opportunities to area school children and other groups. Story time, guided tours, and fishing programs are part of the educational outreach plan; informational learning trunks are also a teacher resource available for check out use. Most programs are provided free of charge; consult the website calendar or call for information regarding these programs.

Sea Center Texas is open Tuesday through Saturday, 9:00 a.m. to 4:00 p.m., and Sunday 1:00 p.m. until 4:00 p.m. They are closed New Year's Day, Easter, Thanksgiving, Christmas Eve and Day, and New Year's Eve. The facility may close for special events or maintenance work; consult the website or call prior to visiting to confirm operating hours.

TEXAS FUN FACT:

The Lightening Whelk is only found in the Gulf Coast, and its shell is the Official State Shell of Texas. The whelks can grow up to a foot long, and the spiral shells open to the left, unlike most spirals that open to the right.

Tyler Municipal Rose Garden

420 Rose Park Drive

Tyler, TX 75702

(903) 531-1212

www.cityoftyler.org/Default.aspx?tabid=590

Welcome to the Rose of Texas! This 14-acre garden represents Tyler's livelihood, and a lovely one at that. In 1900, the major cash crop of East Texas was fruit. When a peach blight destroyed the orchards, the people turned to growing roses. They quickly learned that oil was not all that boomed in Texas, but these little fragrant flowers, too. October 1933 brought the first Texas Rose Festival, celebrating the community's success. By the 1940's, half of America's rose supply was grown within ten miles of Tyler.

The Tyler garden is the largest rose garden in the United States. With 500 rose varieties, and over 38,000 bushes, it is proudly designated as one of the All American Rose Selection test gardens. New breeds are tried for two years, and rated before selection for the general market. Botanists—both professional and amateur—come to photograph, sketch, and smell the new varieties.

Spring and October are best visiting times for blooming flowers, but the Tyler Rose Gardeners work throughout the year to create an appealing place for many to enjoy regardless of the season (even for those without a green thumb!). The Heritage Rose and Sensory Garden is a community of 50 varieties of roses and perennials that bloom throughout the summer. The IDEA garden is just as the name implies—a garden to provide landscaping and plant choice ideas for visitors to take home and use. The Vance Burks Memorial Camellia Garden towers with pine providing shade to the many types of camellias below. Whether in the daylily beds or on hosta-lined trails, around a reflection pool, or under the gazebo, Tyler Rose Garden visitors of any age will find plenty to keep their interest. The Tyler Rose Garden is open daily from dawn until dusk.

OUTSIDE

Alibates National Monument: Flint Quarries

c/o NPS Area Headquarters Building

419 E. Broadway

Fritch, TX 79036

(806) 857-3151

www.nps.gov/alfl

About 40 miles north of Amarillo, Texas Panhandle visitors will find the Alibates National Monument. While the wide open skies of Fritch show visitors what all the songwriting is about, what makes the area special is not necessarily all of the singing cowboys and spacious ranches popular of the region. The history of Alibates goes back as far as 10,000 years.

Like other National Monuments, Alibates recognizes a place of historical significance. However, a specific event is not honored, rather the lasting resource used by man dating back to prehistoric times. Alibates flint quarries within the Canadian River area cap rock tells of a time before "recorded" history.

Flint found in the Alibates is strong, yet brittle, making it the perfect material for arrow and spear heads. Archeological evidence throughout the southwestern American states date Alibates flint tools as far back as 10,000 years, and up until the 1800's. What makes Alibates flint distinguishable from other types is its coloring. Rich tones of maroon, blue and gold marble the mineralized rock; the coloring is distinct to Alibates. No other place in the world has this flint, yet spear and arrow tips are found throughout the region, except at the quarries themselves. So, in a time before malls or even stores, geologists and archeologists believe to have found evidence of trade.

A trip to Alibates National Monument is, well, monumental. Tourists have the opportunity to witness and experience this land in the broad historical sense. While there is no elaborate structure to mark the quarries, making the trek up the canyon side, just as many have done before, is a task well rewarded with a view of literal timeless beauty.

The Alibates Flint National Monument trip is considered moderately strenuous—good hiking boots, weather appropriate clothing and plenty of drinking water are necessities. Tours are Ranger-guided only, and are a combination of driving, walking, and up/down stone hill stair climbing. There are a few rest points along the one-mile trail, and the Ranger willingly stops as needed, but guests should be prepared to move throughout the terrain in order to arrive at the monument. Tours last about two hours and are filled with stories of native flora and fauna, as well as local legends and history. Call the National Park Headquarters in Fritch (also HQ for Lake Meredith) to make tour arrangements. Tours are usually given at 10:00 a.m. and 2:00 p.m.; however extreme temperatures or weather may change or cancel times.

TEXAS FUN FACT:

Alibates is named for Ali Bates, a cowboy who once lived close to a creek by the flint quarries. People named the creek after Bates, and consequently the area inherited the same name.

Amistad National Recreation Area

4121 Veterans Blvd

Del Rio, TX 78840

(830) 775-7491

www.nps.gov/amis

Lake Amistad, named for the Spanish word meaning "friendship," is the product of collaboration between the United States and Mexico. Construction of the dam/reservoir began in 1964; it was complete in 1969. The lake is owned by both countries, and operated by the International Boundary and Water Commission. The U.S. side near Del Rio is a National Recreation Area, commemorating the agreement and alliance between our country and Mexico. The recreation area extends 74 miles up the Rio Grande, 25 miles into Devil's Canyon and 14 miles up the Pecos. Throughout the park, there are opportunities for recreation, and many are offered free of charge.

Visitors to the National Recreation Area should first check in at the Visitor Center. There is a stamping station for National Park Passport collectors, but please know that unlike many National Parks, there is no Junior Park Ranger program for children. While at the center, there are a few exhibits about the natural and cultural resources of the Amistad area, as well as a theater that shows various films at scheduled times, although special arrangements are willingly made. Films include "Transparent Border" about Lake Amistad (available in English and Spanish), "Spirits of the Canyon" about the lower Pecos area rock art, and "A Land of Contrasts" about Big Bend National Park. Informational pamphlets about native plants and animals, activity schedules and calendars, and area maps are also available at the Visitor Center.

Out in the park, guests to Amistad can swim anywhere in the lake, except around boat ramps and the marina area. Please be aware, though, that swimming areas are marked on the park map, and these are the most popular and perhaps safest areas to swim, as no lifeguards are on duty. There are eight picnic areas around the lake as well, and restroom facilities are usually nearby. Driving and hiking are also popular free activities here; the scenery around the lake is quite beautiful. Be cautious of native animals, including javelinas, rattlesnakes, various lizards and the Vinegarroon (see Judge Roy Bean Visitor Center).

The Amistad Dam is also a popular spot, marked midway with a monument celebrating the partnership between the United States and Mexico. The symmetrical monument has the United States flag and bald eagle holding an olive branch, and the Mexican flag with an eagle perched on a prickly pear, serpent in beak. It is an excellent photo opportunity, as visitors can stand in both countries at once.

The Amistad National Recreation Area is open daily, and day use areas close at dark. The Visitor Center is open 8:00 a.m. to 5:00 p.m. daily, but is closed January 1st, Thanksgiving, and December 25th. Boating, hunting, and camping are also available at the ANRA, however, permits are needed for these activities. Consult the website, call, or speak with rangers at the Visitor Center for details and fees for the permits.

TEXAS FUN FACT:

The Mexican flag holds symbolism from the country's early Aztec roots. According to legend, the Aztec gods told the people that their city should be established where they found an eagle, perched on a prickly pear bush, devouring a serpent. The Aztecs saw such this sign near a marsh that is now the main plaza of Mexico City.

Big Thicket National Preserve

6044 FM 420

Kountze, TX 77625

(409) 951-6725

www.nps.gov/bith

Big Thicket National Preserve was recognized as such in 1974 by President Gerald Ford, and is America's first National Preserve. Expanded in 1993, the public land now encompasses over 97,000 acres. Big Thicket provides many opportunities for visitors—recreational and educational. Covering numerous land types, the preserve is not consolidated into one area, but spread throughout the Piney Woods Region and down into the Gulf Coast area near Beaumont. Picnic areas, birding observation sites, horseback and bike paths, hiking trails, canoe/kayak courses, fishing and boating opportunities are spread out on fifteen units are accessible to visitors throughout the year. Some trails are closed during hunting seasons and guests should check with Preserve Headquarters before going to any area units during these times.

The Big Thicket National Preserve provides many Ranger-led programs free of charge; interest levels range from small children through adult. Starting at the Nature Center, informational exhibits tell about the various land types, vegetation and animal life within the preserve's many boundaries. Visitors can watch a 16 minute general information film; an 8-minute film is also available geared more towards child-interests. Either is an enjoyable overview of the preserve properties, sharing the diverse habitats and inhabitants of the Big Thicket area. Interested youth will be happy to know that Big Thicket also participates in the Junior Ranger program (ask for workbooks at the Visitor Center/Headquarters building). Curriculum based programs and activities for teachers are also available, aligned with Texas state learning objectives.

Intriguing to many is the carnivorous plant area in the Turkey Creek Unit. Four out of five American species populate the decked observation area, from floral-tubed pitcher plants to sticky-petaled sundews. If bug-eating plants are not of particular interest, the preserve is also home to animals, animals and more animals—including more than 180 bird species, 50 reptile species and numerous amphibians and mammals. Variation is the key to the Big Thicket; visitors can also enjoy strolls among 85 tree species and over 1,000 different flowering plant types. Maps for each area—physical and interest—are available at the Visitor Center.

The Preserve Visitor Center is open daily from 9:00 a.m. until 5:00 p.m., closed only December 25. Park Rangers recommend visitors allow three days to see all of the preserve; driving, hiking, birding and other maps are available at the Nature Center. However, visits can be as short or long as personal schedules allow, as the list of "things to do" is quite extensive. Hunters and fishermen, please make sure to have a valid Texas license before checking in at Headquarters (fishing is year-round, while free hunting permits for are issued starting the last three weekends in July).

TEXAS FUN FACT:

Boy Scout Eagle Projects provided many of the boardwalks within the Big Thicket National Preserve.

TEXAS FUN FACT:

Big Thicket National Preserve was recognized in 1981 as an International Biosphere Reserve. Only 29 out of 400 U.S. National Parks have this honor. (www.unesco.org)

Cameron Park

University Parks Drive and MLK Drive along the Brazos River

201 West Waco Drive (office)

Waco, TX 76702

(254) 750-8080

www.waco-texas.com/city_depts/parks/cameronpark.htm

Cameron Park was dedicated in 1910, named for the memory of William Cameron. Cameron was a Scottish immigrant, and proved himself a great civic leader of Waco. The original purchase by his family was for 125 acres, but in 1920, they donated enough funds to purchase more land for a total of 416 acres.

The largely undeveloped park runs along the Brazos River, and contains large limestone cliffs formed by the Balcones Fault. One attraction on the cliffs, "Lover's Leap", is named for an Indian legend about a Huaco (Waco) Indian Chief's Daughter, in love with the enemy's son, and forbidden to marry. Preferring death over unhappiness, the lovers, well... leap.

Visitors to Cameron Park have a variety of activities (in addition to local folklore) to choose from. Twenty miles of hiking and biking trails are mapped, named and marked for difficulty—for those who want a casual stroll to daring mountain bikers—there is something for all skill levels. Cameron Park also has two disc golf courses, horse trails, playgrounds, picnic areas, a spray park, boat docks, fishing areas, and a horseshoe complex. Park Rangers offer free courses (registration required) on many activities around the city, including Cameron Park. Call (254) 750-8057 for course information.

The lush canopies of Cameron Park are beautiful, yet easily distracting. The entrances to the park are clearly marked; however, exit sides of the roads are not always labeled as such, so it is easy to find the way out of the park and into a nearby residential area. Informational park attraction signs are posted at each intersection, so lost visitors usually find their way fairly quickly.

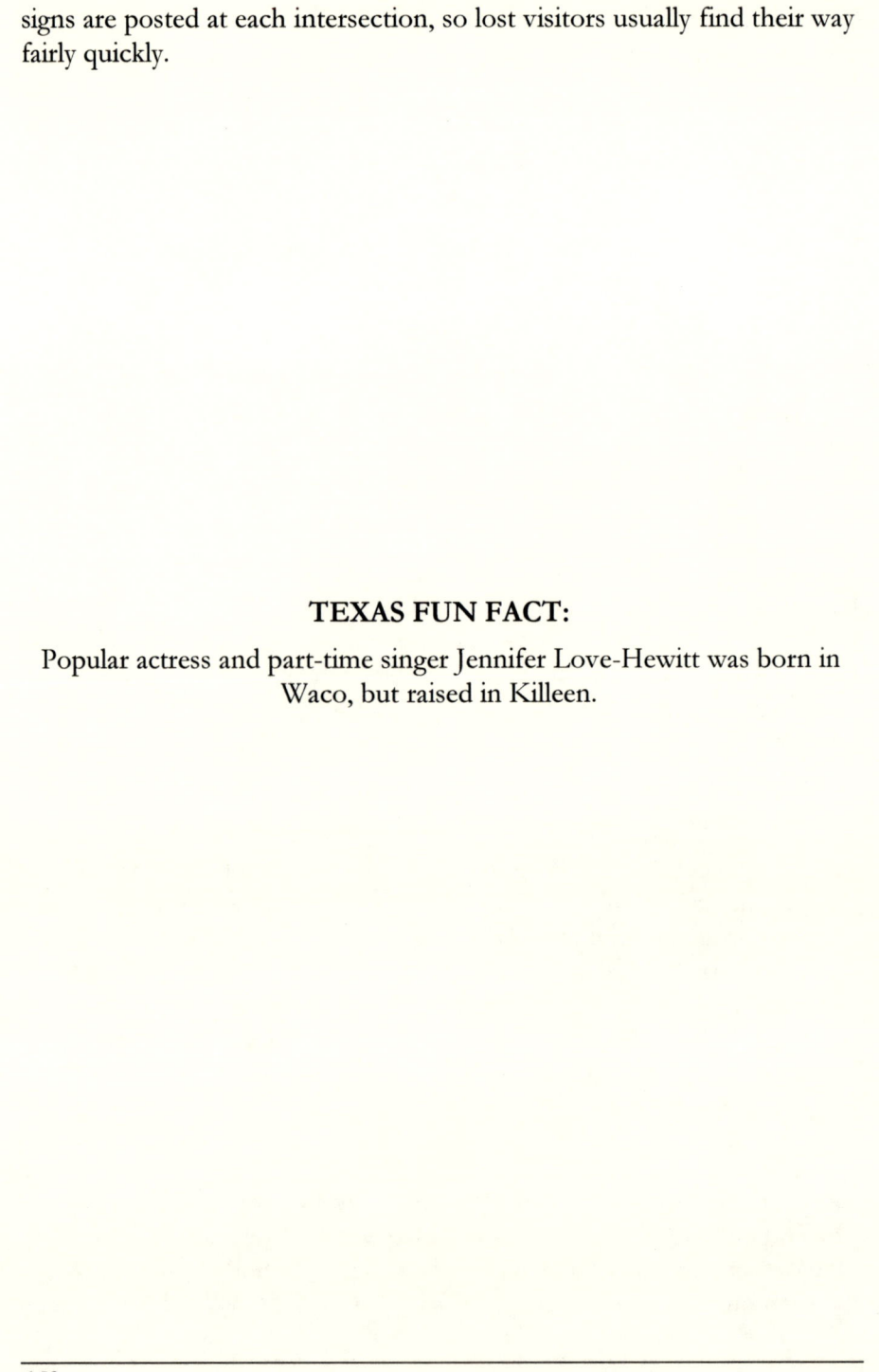

TEXAS FUN FACT:

Popular actress and part-time singer Jennifer Love-Hewitt was born in Waco, but raised in Killeen.

Cibolo Nature Center

140 City Park Rd.

Boerne, TX 78006

(830) 249-4616

www.cibolo.org

The vision of Cibolo Nature Center started as one woman's idea, but it quickly grew to a community-wide project. Great numbers of volunteers have grown the 100-acre park into the preservation and learning center it is today, with goals to educate and entertain while promoting care for the area's land, water, and wildlife.

The Cibolo Nature Center began in 1988, under the leadership of Carolyn Chipman Evans, who convinced Boerne city officials to develop part of the City Park, with aspirations of maintaining the area's natural heritage. The center opened on Earth Day 1990, and has been an integral part of the Boerne Community ever since.

Visitors to the Cibolo Nature Center will find the charming 100-plus year old building used as the Visitor Center. The building was originally a part of the nearby Herff Ranch homestead. Renovated by volunteers, the Visitor Center has hands-on learning displays for children, as well as information about the park and its many offerings of programs and events. Numerous workshops and other activities are available through Cibolo; some are ticketed, while others are "free choice" events. Many of the workshops take place in the newly constructed Lende Learning Center, and extend throughout the park according to subject matter.

The Cibolo Nature Center is home to five trails within four different ecosystems. Close to the center's buildings is the Dinosaur Track-way, a recreation of an 80-foot stretch of Acrocanthosaurus footprints, discovered on the Cibolo property after a 1997 flood. The original tracks are not easily accessible, so they are recreated here for visitors to enjoy. The Woodlands Trail, shaded by oaks, provides shelter to deer, armadillos and raccoons. The Marshland Trail is the hotspot for birdwatchers, while the banks of the Cibolo Creek play host to large, towering cypress, and a creek side picnic area (this is also a popular spot for swimming and catch and release fishing). Native grasses and wildflowers can be seen while strolling down the Native Texas Prairie Trail.

Cibolo Nature Center is a popular birdwatcher "hangout". It is not unusual to see 30-40 different bird types within a two hour visit to the park; a checklist is available in the Visitor Center. Photographs of the park and its inhabitants are welcome, and encouraged. The Cibolo Nature Center is open every day from 8:00 a.m. until dusk; the Visitor Center is also open daily, from 9:00 a.m. until 5:00 p.m.

TEXAS FUN FACT:

Boerne is named after German author and publicist, Ludwig Boerne. Ludwig Boerne is known for his short stories, satire, and political humor.

Cole Park

1526 Ocean Drive

Corpus Christi, TX 78404

(361) 561-0253

www.ccparkandrec.com

Corpus Christi's municipal Cole Park is a 43-acre getaway in a city of getaways. The park has something for everyone, but the talk of the town is the new skate park. Skaters of all abilities are welcome to share the city's newest free attraction—a contoured concrete course on the Corpus Christi coast. It's a big hit, especially for skateboarders (and parents), since most skate parks charge admission. If skills are in need of improvement, free skate lessons are provided on Saturdays for skaters 12 and under (call (361)826-3460 for details).

However, Cole Park's fun doesn't stop at the Skate Park. Also in the park is KidsPlace, an absolutely "ginormous" playground structure. Kids and willing adults can run, jump, climb, crawl, swing, slide, wiggle, and balance in and around the ADA-compliant playground equipment. Around KidsPlace are covered and uncovered patios and picnic tables. The best part? The constant cooling coastal breeze helps keep overheating at a minimum, but still bring lots of water and snacks, as the constant movement on the playground can still be draining.

As if the Skate Park and KidsPlace were not enough, there's still more to this great city park. A lighted fishing pier, restroom facilities, and an amphitheater lure visitors to enjoy the outside. Thursday and Sunday evenings in the summer, the city provides free concerts at the amphitheater; guests only need to bring their own seating and refreshments.

Corpus Christi's Bay Trail runs through Cole Park as part of the 8 miles of trails along the bay's coast. The trail is a popular place for rollerblading, walking, jogging, cycling, and bird watching. The trail also leads to other free city parks, such as Oleander Point (kiteboarding and windsurfing) and McGee Beach (swimming, sunbathing, and picnicking). Bay Trail runs from the ship channel to Cayo de Oso by Texas A & M University Corpus Christi.

TEXAS FUN FACT:

The city of Corpus Christi was named by Catholic Spaniards. The translation from Latin of Corpus Christi is "Body of Christ".

Lanana Creek Trail

c/o Nacogdoches Visitor Center

200 East Main

Nacogdoches, TX 75961

(888) OLDEST TOWN

www.visitnacogdoches.com

Original brainchild of Stephen F. Austin State University's Dr. Frank Abernathy, the Lanana Creek Trail was initially a 1976 United States Bicentennial celebration project. Its popularity continued through to 1986, when public celebrations turned to Texas' Sesquicentennial. Today, it remains still, with no labeled celebration per se, save for the celebration of area history. This land, once traveled by Native Americans, follows Lanana Creek from Main Street (behind Liberty Hall) north two miles to Austin Street.

Lanana Creek Trail is an interestingly mixed hike. Although longer than most walking trails, the trail is considered by most as an "easy walk." The trail has access to many area attractions, yet the remote feeling while strolling has the potential to sweep guests away with the feeling of another time. Path-accessible attractions include Oak Grove Cemetery, the Zion Hill First Baptist Church, Pecan Park, the Children's Garden, SFASU's Mast Arboretum and Ruby Mize Azalea Garden, among others.

A stop at Oak Grove Cemetery can find gravesites of four signers of the Texas Declaration of Independence: Thomas Rusk, Charles Taylor, William Clark, and John Roberts. Directly north on Lanana Street is Zion Hill Baptist Church—home of the oldest African American church in Nacogdoches. The building was built in 1914, but the congregation was founded in 1879. Pecan Park provides various facilities, including restrooms and a playground, and the Children's Park shares playfulness with a waterfall and bronze sculpture reminiscent of the days of Tom and Huck. The Arboretum and Azalea Garden provide area agricultural students study material, and visitors with examples of the natural beauty of East Texas.

Informational maps about Lanana Creek Trail are available at the Nacogdoches Visitor Center at 200 Main or the Liberty Hall entrance to the trail. The trail is open during daylight hours, as are most of the free attractions along the way.

TEXAS FUN FACT:

Nacogdoches is considered to be the oldest town in Texas, with evidence of settlement dating from 10,000 years ago.

Lake Meredith National Recreation Area

103 N. Robey St.

Fritch, TX 79036

(806) 857-3151

www.nps.gov/lamr

In 1947, Texas' Panhandle Water Conservation Authority saw the need for a regular water source in the area. The U.S. Bureau of Reclamation was petitioned; after much persuasion and many years, the Canadian River Municipal Water Authority was born in 1953. Its primary goal was to create a readily available water source for area citizens. By 1960, a contract was signed to build the Sanford Dam, managed under the National Park Service. Not only would the Sanford Dam create Lake Sanford as a water source, but as a recreational facility as well. 1965 brought the final closure of the lake, and normal water deliveries were made in 1968 after the construction of more necessary facilities. One of the early area leaders, A.A. Meredith, was credited for his promotion of the lake project. In 1972, the Sanford Recreation Area was renamed in his honor.

Today, visitors regularly enjoy Mr. Meredith's efforts. The National Recreation Area is over 45,000 acres of canyons, grasslands, and the 10,000 acre reservoir. Land features and plants typical of the region create the oasis in the otherwise dusty terrain; limestone, cottonwood, yucca, mesquite, and prickly pear come together for a picturesque landscape.

Boating is the most popular Lake Meredith sports, but it is by no means the only choice. The National Recreation Area offers hiking, wildlife watching, fishing, hunting, camping and picnic areas. Fishing and hunting both require licenses, and sportsmen must follow park guidelines. Hunting regulations are very specific and are outlined on the website, or hunters can also contact the National Parks Service for a copy of the rules.

Off road vehicle and horseback riding is also approved, and facilities/trails are provided within designated areas only (riders provide own transportation). There are 11 camping sites, and amenities range from primitive (no facilities) to limited (some have chemical toilets or a comfort station with running water). All camping sites are provided free of charge; the only fees in the Recreation Area are for the boat launch and group/social use permits.

Lake Meredith National Recreation Area headquarters building is open 8:00 a.m. to 4:30 p.m. daily from Memorial Day to Labor Day, and Monday through Friday the remainder of the year (closed on major holidays). The park is open 24 hours year round.

TEXAS FUN FACT:

Surprisingly about 10% of Texas' land is actually covered by forest.

Rio Bosque Wetlands Park

10716 Socorro Road

El Paso, TX 79927-1265

(915) 747-8663

www.riobosque.org

The Rio Bosque Wetlands Park is a 372-acre city park on the southeastern side of El Paso. The University of Texas El Paso works through the Center for Environmental Resource Management to recover the ecosystems once found in the river valley. The park, enclosed by irrigation canals on three sides and the Rio Grande River on the other, used to be a wide bend of the Rio Grande River itself. After channelization in the 1930's, the land was under the control of the United States Government (due to the boundary issues with Mexico), but later in 1973, the park was given to the City of El Paso.

Visitors to RBWP have the opportunity to see the area's wildlife and native plants through a set of clearly marked trails. One trail, marked with a frog, is hard paved, wheelchair accessible, and introduces the natural area. The Wetlands, marked by a duck, share the river channel with hikers, and the longest (dragonfly) provides the best opportunity to view the wetlands as a whole. The trails range from 0.6 to 2.4 miles in length. While hiking, visitors may see a variety of native animals, including bullfrogs, snakes, lizards, mice, foxes, beavers, dove, roadrunners, owls, egrets, and hawks. The vegetation of Rio Bosque Wetlands Park is still in early stages of re-growth, and the Center for Environmental Resource Management works to find solutions to bring green back to the valley.

The Visitor Center provides nine different educational brochures for tourists and students about the Rio Bosque area. Visitors are welcome to tour the lands individually; free guided tours are offered twice a month by UTEP, and last about two hours. One of the monthly tours is an overview of the park, its history and the restoration of plants and animals in the region, while the other monthly tour focuses on the various bird species found in the park. The tours cover approximately two miles, and are on primarily level ground. Tour participants meet at the bridge crossing the Riverside Canal.

The Rio Bosque Wetlands Park is open 7 days a week during daylight hours. Trail guides and educational brochures are available outside the Visitor Center if it is closed. Be cautioned that the restroom facilities are closed when no staff are on duty.

TEXAS FUN FACT:

According to internet legend, and the *Tonight Show with Jay Leno*, the El Paso City Council once voted to spend $112,000 to hire a private security firm to guard the city's police station.

MILITARY

Fort Bliss Museums

Bldg. 1735 Marshall Rd.

Fort Bliss, TX 79916-3802

(915) 568-3390

https://www.bliss.army.mil/Museum/fort_bliss_museum.htm

Fort Bliss was first known as "the post opposite El Paso" in 1849. By 1854, it was renamed Fort Bliss, in honor of General Zachary Taylor's chief of staff (and son-in-law) during the Mexican War—Brevet Colonel William Wallace Smith Bliss who had died the year before of yellow fever. The post is now home to the U.S. Army Air Defense Artillery Center and School and all FORSCOM Air Defense Artillery Brigades.

The Fort Bliss Museum is a combination of three areas, together encompassing 108,000 square feet. Information regarding 1857-1900 is housed in the Fort Bliss Museum, sharing about the post's beginnings. The Air Defense Artillery Museum takes the 1900's until present time; numerous examples and explanations of artillery and weapons show changes throughout the years. The museum also contains a replica of "Old Fort Bliss," a gift from the city of El Paso, now used to present bicultural programs about life in the early years of Texas. Visitors can easily spend well over an hour or two learning about the history of the area through the eyes of the military.

A post one-day pass is required to visit the Fort Bliss museums. Photo identification, proof of vehicle registration and insurance are all needed to drive on post. The museums are open Monday through Saturday, 9:00 a.m. until 4:30 p.m. They are closed Sundays and Federal holidays.

Fort Hood

1st Cavalry Division Museum

Bldg. 2218 761st Tank Battalion Ave.

Ft. Hood, TX 76545

(254) 287-3626

http://pao.hood.army.mil/1stCavDiv/museum1.htm

4th Infantry Division Museum

Bldg. 418 761st Tank Battalion Ave.

Ft. Hood, TX 76544

(254) 287-8811

http://pao.hood.army.mil/4ID/museum/museummain.html

Camp Hood was established in 1942 as an armored training center, named in honor of General John Bell Hood (leader of the Civil War's *Hood's Texas Brigade*). The temporary post was designated permanent in 1950, and Fort Hood has now grown into one of the largest military instillations in the world. Included in the various military units are the 1st Cavalry Division and 4th Infantry Division, both of which have museums on post.

The 1st Cavalry Division Museum covers the history of the cavalry from the Civil War, through the formation of the 1st Cavalry Division, up into present day. A First Team soldier greets guests, and gives a short orientation briefing of the museum. Visitors are then able to tour the museum freely at their own pace. Treasure Hunt activity guides are also available for children. Memorabilia, photographs, uniforms, weapons and equipment displays are clearly labeled, and life-sized dioramas help establish a sense of place and time. Outside, an extensive static display of aircraft, armored vehicles and artillery include foreign vehicles as well. The 1st Cavalry Museum is open Monday through Friday, 9:00 a.m. to 4:00 p.m., Saturday 10:00 a.m. until 4:00 p.m., and Sunday noon to 4:00 p.m. The museum is closed New Year's Day, Easter, Thanksgiving, and Christmas Day. On post training holidays, the museum opens at noon and closes at 4:00 p.m. Guided tours can be arranged through the museum office.

The 4th Infantry Division Museum is primarily self-guided tour as well, and follows the division's history from 1917 to present. The tribute to 1st Brigade's capture of Saddam Hussein is an eye opener; a life sized mannequin of Saddam stands next to the actual $750,000 box (sans money) found next to him in the hole where he was captured. A trip to the 4th I.D. Museum Kid Zone allows dress-up time in various military uniforms and accessories, and is always a favorite for the little ones and picture-taking parents.

Outside, the Tank Destroyer monument and exhibit are old favorites. A new favorite, however, is the Fallen Soldier Memorial. A young girl touches the shoulder of a grieving soldier, kneeling before a monument of a friend's boots, helmet and rifle. The 4th Infantry Division Museum is open 9:00 a.m. to 4:00 p.m., Monday through Friday, Saturday 10:00 a.m. until 4:00 p.m., Sunday and holidays noon to 4:00 p.m., and is closed Thanksgiving and Christmas.

Fort Hood visitors will need to go through the Main Gate Visitor Center with driver's license, vehicle registration and proof of insurance to receive a day pass to visit the museums.

TEXAS FUN FACT:

Both the photographer, Stuart Lloyd, and his grandfather, H.C. Lloyd, have been stationed at Fort Hood during their service time in the U.S. Army.

Fort Martin Scott

1606 E. Main Street

Fredericksburg, TX 78624

(830) 997-9895

www.fortmartinscott.com

Fort Houston was built in 1848 on the outskirts of newly established Fredericksburg as an attempt to protect the settlement from area Native Americans. However, the Comanches had already agreed to a treaty (Meusebach-Comanche Treaty) with the German settlers previous to the U.S. Army's intervention efforts, so the fort ended up as a haven for travelers and traders in the area. Fort Houston was renamed Fort Martin Scott in 1849 after Major Martin Scott who was killed in the Battle of Molina del Rey previous to the establishment of the fort. Martin Scott remained an active U. S. Army fort until 1953. During the early 1860's, the area continued on as a meeting place and stopover for new Gillespie County homesteaders, but in 1866 it was abandoned.

In 1870 the Braeutigam family bought the property with the intentions of continuing the social aspect of the area alive, however, the saloon and dance halls were closed in 1884 when Mr. Braeutigam was murdered in an attempted robbery. The property served as fair grounds for the first Gillespie County Fairs from 1881-1888. The Braeutigams sold the property to the City of Fredericksburg in 1959. In 1986, reconstruction of the fort was started by the Fredericksburg Heritage Federation.

Today, fort visitors can share in the experience of what drew the first pioneers to this part of Texas. Moss covered oaks throughout could have easily seen the fort's earlier days, along with Baron's Creek running on the border. The visitor center and reconstructed buildings display artifacts and details about the life during the operational times of the fort.

The buildings are open Tuesday through Saturday 10:00 a.m. to 5:00 p.m. There is an informational self guided tour map available at the visitor center, and lucky tourists will find some time to speak with one of the knowledgeable docents. Fort grounds are accessible after hours.

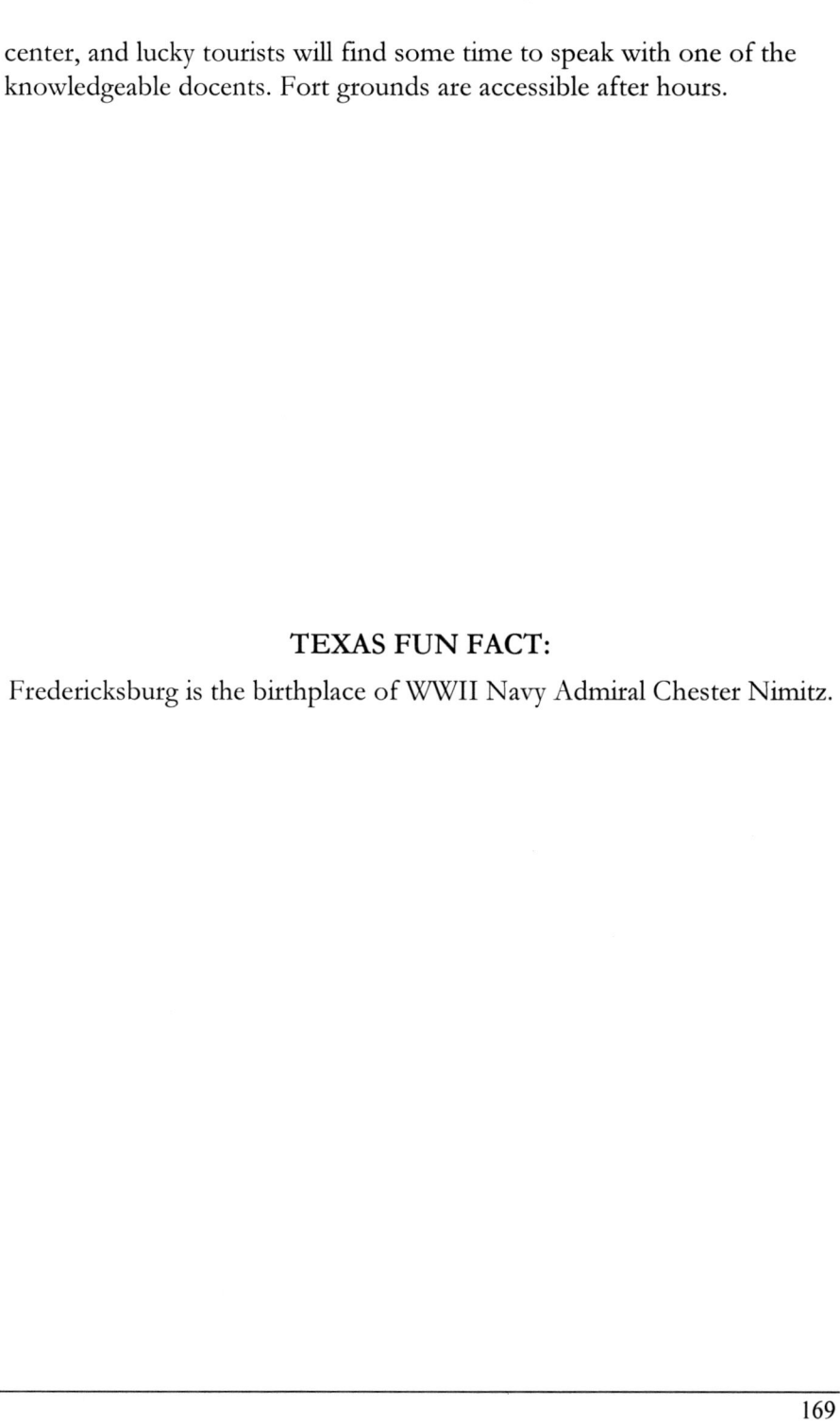

TEXAS FUN FACT:

Fredericksburg is the birthplace of WWII Navy Admiral Chester Nimitz.

Fort Sam Houston: Army Medical Department Museum

2310 Stanley Rd. Bldg. 1046

Fort Sam Houston, TX 78234

(210) 221-6358

http://ameddregiment.amedd.army.mil/museum2/index.htm

The Army's first medical museum was founded primarily to serve as a research facility in Washington, D.C. in 1862. After a few other moves, the museum relocated for the last time to Fort Sam Houston in 1946. Once known as the National Museum of Health and Medicine of the Armed Forces Institute of Pathology at Walter Reed Army Medical Center, the facility is now called the U.S. Army Medical Department Museum. The present building was built in 1989, with respect to the Spanish Revival architectural style of the area. The glass enclosed breezeway and court fountain are enjoyable details to this facility.

The USAMDM emphasizes the role and importance of the Army's medical contributions. Medical artifacts, memorabilia, uniforms, vehicles, photos, and equipment are displayed, organized by conflict. The exhibit areas are defined by color and design while opposing county's flags hang from overhead beams. Artistic portrayals of soldiers, officers and their mission emphasize each area, bringing a sense of understanding and compassion to the lives these men and women choose to lead.

The USAMDM also offers short films for viewing visitors, covering the span of the Army Medical Department's history. Outside, more vehicles are displayed, including a Korean hospital train, helicopter and field ambulance used to transport patients.

The U.S. Army Medical Department Museum is open Tuesday through Saturday, 10:00 a.m. to 4:00 p.m., and is closed Federal holidays. Occasionally there are special events scheduled; contact the website or call for details. The Fort Sam Houston visitor gate is the Harry Wurzbach entrance. Visitors will need photo identification, vehicle registration, and proof of insurance to drive on post.

Texas Military Forces Museum at Camp Mabry

Building 6

2200 W. 35th

Austin, TX 78703

(512) 782-5659

www.texasmilitaryforcesmuseum.org

www.kwanah.com

Camp Mabry was established in the 1890's as a summer field exercise camp for the Texas Volunteer Guard. Now known as the Texas National Guard, soldiers of this institution have participated in major conflicts throughout Texas' history. The Texas Military Forces Museum was dedicated in 1992 in Camp Mabry's building 6 (1918 mess hall), to commemorate the bravery and dedication of those who served in this capacity.

The Texas Military Forces Museum timelines wars from the Texas War for Independence to present-day 49th Armored Division's involvement in Bosnia. The facility includes numerous battle dioramas, uniforms, photographs, equipment and weapons from each major war, as well as personal accounts, stories or biographies of outstanding soldiers and officers. A separate exhibit pays respect to Texas veterans of all branches who have earned the Medal of Honor.

The TMFM also has an extensive collection of "enemy" (changing definition) gear: Mexican, Union, German, Japanese, Italian and Vietnamese items include uniforms, weapons, personal items and equipment. A large collection of weapons, aircraft, field artillery and armored vehicles, both American and foreign, is spread throughout the museum and its grounds.

Photo identification is necessary to enter Camp Mabry, and the Texas Military Forces Museum is open Wednesday through Sunday from

10:00 a.m. until 4:00 p.m. Free tours include the museum and the Thomas S. Bishop All Faiths Chapel, a structure built by members of the State Military Forces built in 1976 using no government funds.

TEXAS FUN FACT:

Although Texas is very large, 70 % of the state's population actually lives within 200 miles of Austin.

Texas Panhandle War Memorial
4101 S. Georgia
Amarillo, TX 79118
(806) 354-9779

The Texas Panhandle War Memorial is a tribute to fallen war heroes, who have given their lives in service to our country. Giant marble monoliths account the names of Texas Panhandle residents from each war; together the monoliths encircle an incredibly lively and colorful flower garden. Three flags tower over the center of the garden: U.S.A., Texas and POW-MIA. To the memorial's rear is a bell tower that rings throughout the day, reminding all of the sacrifice made by the service men and women.

A meditation tree is to the side, as is a memorial museum. A few items are displayed from various local veterans, and the museum usually has a volunteer available to answer any questions or simply reminisce and compare military experience with visitors. The museum facility is rather small, but the experience inside is immeasurable. Plans for expansion mirror the popularity of the park and importance the community places on the family members and friends who have fought for our country.

The Texas Panhandle War Memorial is visible at all times, and volunteers come as regularly as possible, especially during the regular work week. The memorial is simply picturesque—an incredible opportunity for beautiful photographs. The TPWM Foundation works with the community, raising all money for the memorial (no governmental funding) and performing various service projects as needed in the area. Clearly, these veterans' hearts began in service to their country, and have continued on in service to their community.

HISTORICAL PLACES

1861 Custom Home

502 20th St.

Galveston, TX 77550

(409) 763-1877

www.galvestonhistory.org/1861_US_Custom_House.asp

Galveston's Customs House is a tower of strength and tenacity, flexibility and triumph. It has survived and overcome the effects of war, storms, fire, explosions, and disinterest. Important from the very beginning, focus of the building shifted from collecting tariffs for the United States Government, to eventually providing research material into the city's past

The Custom House was built between 1860 and 1861, in an incredible 114 days. The construction company, Blaisdell and Emerson, were afraid of Texas' secession, and finished quickly for fear that the United States would not follow through with payment for a state with which they were at war. Ammi B. Young's Renaissance Revival design required cast iron pieces shipped from New York. The pieces were designed, completed, shipped and put together with the red-brown brick to make the first and longest standing federal building in Texas—all in 114 days.

Since its construction, the house has survived many human and natural disasters: the Battle of Galveston in the Civil War, the 1885 Galveston Fire, 1900 Great Storm, 1960 Hurricane Carla, 1978 boiler explosion, and Hurricane Rita in 2005. During Rita, three buildings across the street burned in the evacuated town; if not for dedicated firefighters who stayed behind, the 1861 Custom House would not have survived. The Custom House has served as a federal customs building, Union soldier post, Confederate soldier post, Post Office, federal courthouse, and is now the headquarters building for the Galveston Historical Foundation (since 1999—after being unused since 1985).

Today, the Galveston Historical Foundation works with most of the historically significant properties in Galveston. The Preservation Resource Center is on the first floor of the 1861 Custom House, and provides on-site research materials of the properties the GHF manages. Walking into the house, visitors see the original cast iron double return stairway in the H-shaped building. Though the building is mostly offices for the GHF, visitors can enjoy details from the past; included are the courthouse-era prisoner holding pen that now serves as the GHF director's office and the decorative emblem of the United States outside on the second floor triangular gable (imagined not popular with the Confederate soldiers).

The 1861 Custom House is open from 8:30 a.m. to 5:00 p.m., Monday through Friday. Within the Galveston Historical Foundation, visitors can pick up a "Places to Visit Map" with marked properties under GHF's care. On the map, note the 1880 Garten Verein, a German Social Club from the 19th century. The historical hangout hosts a Dancing Pavilion and lovely gardens, both free for tourists to view if an event is not planned. The Galveston County History Museum is within a few blocks—east on E for three blocks, then turn north on Market (see www.galvestonhistory.org or call (409)766-2340 for information).

TEXAS FUN FACT:

The Galveston Historical Foundation is the second largest historical society in the United States, second only to the United States Capitol Historical Society.

Carson County Square House Museum Complex

5th and Elsie (Hwy 207)

Panhandle, TX 79068

(806) 537-3524

www.squarehousemuseum.org

The Square House in Panhandle found its beginnings as a headquarters building of the Niedringhaus Brothers' N Bar N Ranch—one of the first and most important ranches in Carson County. The wooden frame house was built from Dodge City wood, hauled by ox-cart to Panhandle in the late 1880's. Today, the restored house is the center of the Carson County Square House Museum Complex, including 21 structures covering the history of various times in the area's history.

Visitors to the complex will find many choices on the grounds, but the Square House itself is most striking. The house is 24'x24'—square as the name implies. A rooftop captain's walk tops this lovely white colonial, and visitors will not find it surprising to learn of the numerous Texans who called this place home (if even for a short while).

The museum complex also includes a pioneer dugout, a Santa Fe caboose, recreations of a bank and blacksmith shop, a wildlife hall, farm and ranch exhibits, and even an Eclipse Windmill. The complex is also home to the 1912 Conway Community Church and one of the largest collections of Native American art in Texas. Over 10,000 artifacts, documents, photos, guns, sculptures and other items are a part of the celebration of man and time—from mammoth hunters, through ranching, railroads and the oil boom, right into Carson County's connection with the space program.

The Carson County Square House Museum Complex also has an extensive outreach program, with numerous teaching trunks and videotapes for educators. Consult the website or call for information on these programs. The museum complex is open 9:00 a.m. to 5:00 p.m., Monday through Saturday and 1:00 p.m. to 5:00 p.m. on Sunday. They are closed New Year's Day, Easter, Thanksgiving, and Christmas. Tours are self guided, but free group tours can be arranged; please call first.

TEXAS FUN FACT:

Conway Community Church's hometown is nine miles south of Panhandle, in Conway. Although the church is now in Panhandle, tourists may enjoy a view of the historical "Route 66" (a.k.a. I-40 in Conway). This town is now home to the *VW Bug Ranch*—similar to the *Cadillac Ranch* west of Amarillo (also on I-40).

Durst-Taylor Historic House and Gardens

304 North St.

Nacogdoches, TX 75961

(936) 560-4443

www.visitnacogdoches.org

The property holding the Durst-Taylor House (also called Acosta-Taylor House), traces back to the later 1700's, and was first owned by Anders de Acosta, Mexican settler in early Nacogdoches. Acosta sold the house to Joseph Durst in 1826, starting a string of ownership until landing in the hands of Lawrence Taylor in 1870. Between Durst and Taylor, the house was occupied by San Jacinto veteran Isaac Burton, Delegate to the 1875 Constitutional Convention Bennett Blake, Thomas Rusk, and William Oohiltree, a member of the Provisional Congress of the Confederacy, among others. Although ownership changed often, Lawrence Taylor's family remained in the house from first purchase in 1870 until 1989.

Architectural interests will find a home at the Durst-Taylor House. The two story parlor plan house is typical of the 1820-1850 era homes. Specific detail interests are the differing mantles on each level (Federal Survival on first floor, Greek Revival on second), gable-end chimneys, and paneled shutters. The property tour begins at the barn, and includes a blacksmith workshop, a smokehouse, and heritage gardens. The tour involves a bit of walking; comfortable shoes are recommended.

Guides at the Durst-Taylor Historic Home and Gardens are quite knowledgeable and provide excellent insight into the history of Nacogdoches and lives of her early settlers. The Visitor Center, located in the Barn, is open from 10:00 a.m. until 4:00 p.m., Tuesday through Saturday. The DTHHG is a designated State Archaeological Landmark.

Gonzales Historical Tours

Start at Chamber of Commerce/ Old Jail Museum

414 St. Lawrence Street

Gonzales, TX 78629

(830) 627-6532

www.gonzalestexas.com/visitor/tours.asp

When Sam Houston heard of the defeat at the Alamo in March 1836 from Susannah Dickenson, he ordered all Texans to join him in the retreat to the Colorado River. The city of Gonzales, where Houston received the news, was burned and the occupants fled to safety, starting the "Runaway Scrape." Many people died on this journey from their home due to illness coupled with exhaustion, and were often buried in the same spot in which they fell.

After the April victory over Santa Anna at San Jacinto, many citizens of Gonzales returned to their home, determined to rebuild. They did, using the original plan for the city set by the Mexican government in 1832. Although the city plan remained the same, the houses built by citizens in newly booming cattle and cotton businesses were extravagant—large and ornate. Frame homes were built from cypress—trees not native of the area, but brought from Florida and Louisiana by oxcart. German artisans traveled through the area, often living with a family long enough to complete intricate woodwork such as a hand carved walnut staircase. There was an apparent pride in rebuilding the "Birthplace of Texas" as a more glorified state than before.

Gonzales is the only town in Texas that still has the original Mexican city plan in place. To date, Gonzales has more than 80 historical properties documented—plantation homes, Victorian mansions, cottages, churches, stores, the courthouse, jail—all within the town's center. The Gonzales Chamber of Commerce, located in the Old Jail Museum, has walking and driving tour plans, routes plotted and specific directions to points of interest throughout the city. While visitors are allowed to tour inside homes only on specific ticketed event dates (many are still inhabited), any architectural fan will enjoy the beauty of the historical buildings from the outside. The town has taken great care in labeling each home built before 1916 on the outside, and provides a brief description or history about the building in the walking/driving tour maps. Visitors learn about the escape of Bonnie and Clyde from the Alcalde Hotel and see the first house to use natural gas. Homes of early pioneers, lumbermen, bankers, and cattle barons, including the Houston brothers, are included on the tour as well. The "Sam Houston Oak" is also on the tours, as the site where Houston gathered the troops and shared his plans to escape Gonzales after he learned about the Alamo defeat.

The Gonzales Chamber of Commerce is open Monday through Friday, 8:00 a.m. to 5:00 p.m., Saturday 9:00 a.m. to 4:00 p.m. and Sunday 1:00 p.m. until 4:00 p.m.

TEXAS FUN FACT:

Texans have adopted the Nine-banded armadillo as the official state small mammal, while the Texas longhorn takes the prize for the official large mammal of Texas.

Guenther House

205 East Guenther St.

San Antonio, TX 78204

(210) 227-1061

www.guentherhouse.com

Guenther House is the 1860 home of Pioneer Flour's founding family. Hilmar Guenther came to America in 1848 with a belief that he should "seize the opportunity that presents itself." By 1851, he had built a flour mill in Fredericksburg (C.H. Guenther & Son, Inc.), but drought forced him to sell the mill and relocate next to the San Antonio River in 1859. The next year, he built the house for his growing family. Business boomed, and he renamed the mill Pioneer Flour Mills in 1898. The business is still owned by the family and is the oldest family-owned mill continuing to operate in the United States.

In 1902, Guenther's youngest son, Erhard, became president of the company and remodeled the family home, developing the character of the building through design.

Located in the King William Historical District, the Guenther House is no longer a home to the Guenther family. The house went through one more transformation in 1988 into the restaurant and museum that it is today, with much respect to the original structure and design of the house.

The one room museum shows a collection of mill memorabilia, including baking accessories and cookie cutters. In particular, the collection of anniversary Dresden plates given to customers before World War II is of interest to collectors (although not for sale). German influence on the house is apparent in the Victorian parlor, boasting the original Stuttgart piano owned by the Guenther family. The restaurant is worth popping in for a view of the Art Nouveau décor, including the copper and alabaster light fixtures of Chinese dragons, lily pads and lotus blossoms.

Visitors to Guenther House are welcome to visit any of the three floors during operating hours (7:00 a.m. until 4:00 p.m. daily), unless a room is reserved for a private event.

TEXAS FUN FACT:

Partly built to attract an NFL football team to San Antonio, the Alamo Dome has only been the full time home for a professional football team for one year. That team was the now defunct San Antonio Texas of the Canadian Football League.

Independence Tours
Intersection of Hwy 50 and Hwy 390
Brenham, TX 77833

C/O Independence Preservation Trust
20 Briar Hollow Lane
Houston, TX 77027-2893
(713) 626-8050
www.independencetx.com

Independence was founded in 1835 as a Mexican government land grant. Ironically, after Texas' freedom from Mexico, the town became the center of religious and educational activity for the new Republic of Texas. Baylor College opened in 1846 as a co-ed learning facility, only to be split into separate male/female colleges by 1851. Independence Baptist Church, an integral part and influence of the college, is the site of Sam Houston's baptism in 1854. By 1880, railroads had overlooked Independence. Consequently, the increasingly difficult transportation issues turned the college administration's eyes toward Waco for the male college (now Baylor University) and Belton for the females (now the University of Mary Hardin-Baylor). The once center attraction of Texas soon dwindled to a memory.

Today, Independence remains small; the town is officially part of Brenham, although it is about 14 miles north of the city. Well over 125 years since the bustle of early Texas, the countryside remains beautiful. It is easy to see why Independence was chosen; large live oaks populate the once crowded space. Many of the buildings from that time have long since disappeared, yet some remain. The best place to find a comprehensive map is on the listed website, but information about the buildings is also available through the Washington County Visitor's Bureau found at 314 S. Austin, Brenham, TX 77833, (979) 836-3695.

The one-mile walking tour includes several buildings of significance. The Baylor male campus site on Windmill Hill is now known as Baylor Park, dedicated in March 2006. University landmarks in the park include the burial site of Judge R.E.B. Baylor, for whom the University is named. The Robertson House, now a private residence, was once home to General Jerome Robertson—active in the Texas Revolution and Civil War. The 1835 Adobe House reflects the pre-revolution Mexican architectural influence, and was once the office of the first Chief of Justice of the Republic of Texas. Mrs. Sam Houston's House was where Margaret returned to live with her children after Sam died. Other buildings include a cotton gin and general store.

The Independence Driving Tour includes the walking tour sites, as well as the pre-Civil War Seward Plantation, the old town square, the Groves of Independence, Old Baylor Park (site for female college). Two churches, Independence Baptist and Liberty Baptist, stem from the congregational split of former slaves after the Civil War. The original church, Independence Baptist, is home to the Texas Baptist Museum, open Tuesday through Saturday, 9:00 a.m. until 4:00 p.m. (free admission). Restored early Texas homes are also on the trail: the Coles Cabin and a dog-trot style log cabin. Free tours of these homes are given in April and May; call (979) 830-0230 for tour details. Some of the other buildings on either trail are available for inside sightseeing; the general store continues to operate, and the Seward Plantation charges admission to visit inside. Other buildings are private residential or office spaces now. However, there is plenty opportunity for picnicking, hiking and experiencing the atmosphere of the once-center of Texas activity.

TEXAS FUN FACT:

A yellow fever epidemic hit Independence in 1867, taking Margaret Houston and her two younger daughters victim. They were not taken to Huntsville to rest with Sam, but buried immediately, for fear of spreading the disease. They are buried across from the Independence Baptist Church next to Margaret's mother, Nancy Moffette Lea.

La Villita

South Alamo @ Riverwalk

San Antonio, TX

(210) 207-8610

www.lavillita.com

www.thesanantonioriverwalk.com

San Antonio's first neighborhood, La Villita, was the originally a settlement for soldiers stationed at Mission San Antonio de Valero (otherwise known as the Alamo). From 1795 until 1809, the area was known as Pueblo de Valero. In 1809, the area including the missions and smaller villages combined to make the now-known San Antonio. La Villita is the site where Santa Anna staged troops during the battle of the Alamo.

Immigrants from Germany and France in the 1850s brought a new face to La Villita. Property was bought and new structures replaced the old *palisadoes* (timber shacks with plastered insides). Even through additions and renovations over the next 150 years, the charming European architecture remains true to the heritage of La Villita.

Former San Antonio Mayor Maury Maverick's vision for the preservation of La Villita came through in 1939, when the city worked together to restore the area, renaming buildings and streets to reflect the pan-American spirit. La Villita was recognized as a National Historic Place in 1972.

Today, many of the buildings in La Villita house craftsmen and artists of all sorts: stained glass, glass blowing, metal art, ceramics, pottery, candles, paintings, sculptures, and more. Visitors are welcome to browse through the galleries in the historic buildings while enjoying the quaint atmosphere. The Little Church, built in 1879, is exactly as the name implies; however, members of the congregation are happy share their treasure with passers-by. The stained glass cross on the south wall is worth the visit.

The north side of La Villita attaches to the San Antonio Riverwalk at the Arneson River Theater. Various community events are scheduled at the theater throughout the year. The Riverwalk, or Paseo del Rio, is filled with music, historical buildings, restaurants, and shops. Strolling the Riverwalk is also free and a perfect way to experience the culture of San Antonio.

Visitors are able to view historical buildings at any time; maps are available at the Chamber of Commerce and online. See websites for details about specific attractions of La Villita and the Riverwalk.

TEXAS FUN FACT:

During World War II, the American Red Cross operated its war programs from La Villita.

Polly's Chapel
CR Privilege Creek off SH 16
Bandera, TX 78003

Hill Country visitors often enjoy a simple drive through the countryside, to experience the landscape known for the area. A trip to Polly's Chapel can provide one of Texas' "scenic drives" with a historically significant, albeit remote, end in mind. Just on the east side of Privilege Creek near Bandera, the county road of the same name displays a small white wooden sign, simply stating: "Polly's Chapel, 3 miles." Curious travelers have often happened upon this attraction, finding it well worth the time investment, although the drive seems a bit longer than three miles itself. The paved county road cuts through hills, trees, and pastures, passing private property and ranches until it eventually turns gravel. The creek is crossed three times before coming upon the next indication of the right track is found, another white wooden sign:

"⬅ Polly's Cemetery, Polly's Chapel➡"

A rocky trip to the right finds a small chapel and wooden cross leaned up against a neighboring tree, as well as a Texas Historical Commission Marker that briefly explains the life of Jose' Policarpo Rodriguez.

The chapel came later in Policarpo's life. Born in Mexico in 1829, Polly found his first purpose in life as a scout for the Whiting and Smith expedition in 1849. The westward trip from San Antonio to El Paso was long and through Indian Territory; Polly helped improve the trip back with a shorter, more direct route. His route was soon used as the primary road between the cities.

In 1858, Polly purchased 360 acres in Bandera County on Privilege Creek, the land around his marked areas today. The settlement flourished under his leadership and the town grew to over 300 and included a country store and post office. By 1912, two years before Polly's death, the post offices had closed and most residents had moved on to larger cities.

During the Civil War, he was offered a commission in the CSA, but turned it down in lieu of serving as a private in the Bandera Home Guards near the Privilege Creek settlement. By 1878, Polly had converted to Methodism and had earned a license to preach, finding yet another mission in his life.

In 1882, Polly and the town's residents hand built a chapel out of native stone—this is Polly's Chapel. The simple structure (now equipped with ceiling fans) is where Polly found home. Until his death in 1914, he ministered to the community through this building. Today, group tours are given through various hill country communities; its quaintness and clean architectural lines, along with Polly's story, draw enough visitors to necessitate a covered pavilion of picnic tables. Down the road (past the sign) is Polly's Cemetery, where he lays under the big cedar tree on the left front side of the garden. A large historical marker sites his grave as an important Texan throughout his life.

TEXAS FUN FACT:

Bigfoot is a Texan! Since the 1960's there have been hundreds of sightings of the legendary creature. Most sightings have been in the area of Caddo Lake.

Sam Houston Regional Library and Research Center
1848 Gillard-Duncan House
1883 Norman House
Jean & Price Daniel House

650 FM 1011

Liberty, TX 77575-0310

(936) 336-8821

www.tsl.state.tx.us/shc

Although the Sam Houston Regional Library and Research Center is primarily focused on the research aspect of history preservation, there is something to be said for the buildings on the grounds of our first president's library. The 1848 and 1883 houses each preserve very distinct styles in Texas history, while the Daniel House highlights the lives of the former Governor and First Lady, Price and Jean Daniel.

The 1848 Gillard-Duncan House, one of the oldest houses in southeast Texas, came to the Library grounds in 1980. It was built in memory of the Red River Valley homes in Louisiana by Dr. Edward and Mrs. Emma Gillard out of native cypress and pine. The unusual two-story stresses the importance of education to the Gillards with an upstairs school room. Original pieces furnish the home that also includes an extra "traveler's room" and an enclosed stairway. Unusual as it was for the time, visitors will find that the old world charm is apparent in this well preserved relic. The 1893 Norman House, while more typical of the times, remains a classic with front columns to complete the Greek Revival style home. Symmetrical rooms mirror across a central hall with no indoor amenities. The Norman home came to the SHRLRC in 1994, and now houses changing exhibits about early home life in Texas.

The Jean and Price Daniel House, while a considerable amount younger than the other two structures, pays homage to its previous owners. The Prices had the house built in 1982; the outside is patterned after the original plans of the 1854 Texas Governor's Mansion in Austin. The family donated the land and building to Texas State Library and Archives

Commission, and by 1998, it was completely owned by the state. The house preserves the library, artifacts, and documents about the Daniels' public service to Texas and America amid the parquet flooring and crystal lighting. Price Daniel, a native Texan, held more high state elected positions of anyone in Texas' history, including Texas Attorney General, U.S. Senator, Director if U.S. Emergency Preparedness, and Governor of Texas (among others). While First Lady of Texas, Jean established the Texas Governor's Mansion Historical Collection in Austin—an inventoried catalog of items in the mansion. Together, they authored books two books about public service buildings and homes.

The Sam Houston Regional Library and Research Center is located three miles north of Liberty on FM 1011, and signs mark the way to the center. The houses are open for tours and viewing 9:00 a.m. until 4:00 p.m., Monday through Friday. The Research Center is open Monday through Friday, 8:00 a.m. to 5:00 p.m., and Saturday 9:00 a.m. until 4:00 p.m. The Center includes manuscripts, documents, journals, Indian artifacts, and an assortment of Alabama and Coushatta Indian baskets. There are also a number of photographs of Sam Houston and the Jean Lafitte Journal depicting the life of the legendary Gulf of Mexico pirate.

TEXAS FUN FACT:

Sam Houston is the only person in American history to have been elected and serve as the Governor of two different states (Texas & Tennessee).

Sterne-Hoya Home

211 S. Lanana

Nacogdoches, TX 75961-5148

(409) 560-5426

www.visitnacogdoches.org

The Sterne-Hoya Home, the oldest structure in Nacogdoches still on its original site, is much more than appearances let on. Certainly, the 1830 dog-trot style building is immaculately decorated—one parlor is restored with early Texas décor, as when the Sterne family inhabited it, while another remembers the Hoyas with Victorian furnishings. The stone-walled wine cellar's cornerstone dates 1845; few other changes have been made to the original structure. Only two families have lived in this house before its donation to the City of Nacogdoches in 1958 for use as a public library. Although these facts and the preservation of the home are impressive enough, the history the building contains makes a visit almost necessary to Texas history connoisseurs.

Nicholas Adolphus Sterne built the home in 1830 for his new bride, Eva Catherine. Sterne, a well-known merchant in the area, quickly became involved with Texas' revolutionary efforts. Sam Houston, in order to become a land owner under Mexican law, was baptized Catholic in Sterne's home; Eva Catherine was his godmother. Nicholas Sterne continued allegiance to Texas—he recruited and financed two companies of volunteers from New Orleans in 1835 to fight at the Alamo. He later worked under General Rusk as a captain of the volunteer army that fought at the 1839 Battle of the Neches in the Cherokee War, and went on to become a Texas State Representative and Senator.

Many visitors frequented the house, including Sam Houston, Thomas Rusk, Davy Crockett, and Charles Stanfield Taylor (Texas Declaration of Independence signer). Cherokee Chief Bowl negotiated a peace treaty within these walls with Sam Houston in 1836, exchanging amicable relations between the Native American tribes and the Texans during the Revolution for the promise of East Texas land possession after the war.

Seventeen years after her husband's death, Eva Catherine Sterne sold the house to her neighbor, Joseph Von der Hoya, another German immigrant and settler. Hoya came to Nacogdoches in 1836 to become a farmer and land owner; he eventually fathered many important citizens in Nacogdoches. His granddaughters donated the home to Nacogdoches in 1958.

The Sterne-Hoya Home is open from 10:00 a.m. until 4:00 p.m. Tuesday through Saturday. Thirty minute guided tours are offered, and prove to be quite informative and enjoyable for many age groups. The house retains artifacts from the time periods of the two owners, and also continues as a library. The "Texana Collection" provides information on local and Texas history, while the "Jewel Norwood Tifford Children's Collection" contains many children's classics. The Sterne-Hoya Home is on the National and Texas Registries of Historic Places and is designated as a State Archeological Landmark.

TEXAS FUN FACT:

Sam Houston's Catholic baptism name was Samuel Pablo. He was later baptized as an adult at the Baptist Church in Independence.

TEXAS FUN FACT:

Chief Bowl's peace treaty was later rebuked by the Senate of the Republic of Texas. Bowl considered taking up sides with those who spoke of a Mexican reinvasion, but President Lamar banned the tribes from Texas. Chief Bowl died in 1839 at the Battle of the Neches.

The Paramount

352 Cypress Street

Abilene, TX 79601

(325) 676-9620

www.paramount-abilene.org

In 1928, local wholesale grocer H.O. Wooten began construction of Abilene's Paramount Theatre. Completely vested in his project, he paid cash for its completion after 1929's Black Monday. The theatre soon became a haven for Abilene and her surrounding city, as movie-going was a prominent form of entertainment during the Depression. Soldiers training at Camp Barkley during World War II often visited as well, often entertained not only by the movies, but manager Wally Aiken's well-known promotional stunts as well.

By the 1970's, the Paramount's popularity dwindled. She was scheduled for demolition, but the Abilene Preservation League came and saved the building that had provided emotional respite for so many in the past. The Paramount is now registered as a National Historic Place. After a generous donation (from an anonymous fan), the theatre was restored in 1986. The Paramount now hosts movies (current and classic), live theatre and musical performances. When performances are not scheduled, the building is available for private party rentals.

Abilene visitors are welcome to stop by the Paramount any afternoon from 1:00 p.m. until 5:00 p.m. Checking in through the original designed (restored) box office, informational brochures are available that share the history and structural details of this door to the past. Inside, guests walk into a two-story lobby, decorated in 1930's style—Roman arches, hand-blown glass chandeliers, brass statues, grand staircases leading to the balcony, and an intricately detailed carpet. Large portraits display local theatre icons—H.O. Wooten, Wally Aiken, and Abilene High School drama teacher, Ernest Sublet. The identity of the woman's portrait remains a mystery; she is affectionately referred to as the "Paramount Ghost." Inside the auditorium, rich reds and deep yellows warmly welcome spectators to another world, covered by a twinkling ceiling sky. Although the projection, light and sound technologies provide a more up-to—date experience, the essence and feeling of the Paramount will take visitors back—surely satisfying Mr. Wooten's desire to provide entertainment for many years. If he only knew.

TEXAS FUN FACT:

Abilene was founded for the purpose of serving as a shipping location for livestock along the Texas and Pacific Railway.

Tyrrell Historical Library
695 Pearl Street

Beaumont, TX 77704-3827

(409) 833-2759

The Tyrrell Historical Library found its beginnings as the First Baptist Church of Beaumont in 1903. The congregation outgrew the Romanesque-Gothic building in a short twenty years, and by 1923 it was purchased by local philanthropist Captain William Tyrrell. Tyrrell donated the building to the city of Beaumont for use as a public library, in memory of his wife, Helen. The library opened in 1926, and was used as such until 1974 when a new public library was built to serve the city's expanding needs. The building then became the Tyrrell Historical Library, and went through repairs and restoration in the 1980's. The Tyrrell Library is registered as a Texas Historical Landmark, National Historic Place, and is recipient of the Lucille Terry Preservation Award in 1999.

Tyrrell visitors are greeted with a "please sign in" and a "what can I help you find?" While the Tyrrell Historical Library is primarily a resource for genealogy studies, history enthusiasts will enjoy the extensive historical collection of Texas and local history that line the stained-glass windowed walls. Architecture buffs will enjoy Alonzo N. Dawson's limestone mixed-Richardsonian design, complete with Norman stair towers. The library also shares historical art, photographs, yearbooks, scrapbooks, exhibits and microfilmed newspapers. Clever yoked lamps illuminating the large reading desks encourage study of the past or enjoyment of a days-gone-by story. Librarians and volunteers eagerly address any questions with the "Windows on the Past, Doors to the Future" attitude of this castle-like monument.

The Tyrrell Historical Library provides patrons with many genealogy services—from free access internet research programs to free classes—all to encourage people to get to know themselves by learning about family and community. The library is open Tuesday 8:30 a.m. until 8:00 p.m. and Wednesday through Saturday 8:30 a.m. until 5:30 p.m. Please call head archivist with specific collection inquiries if researching a particular subject.

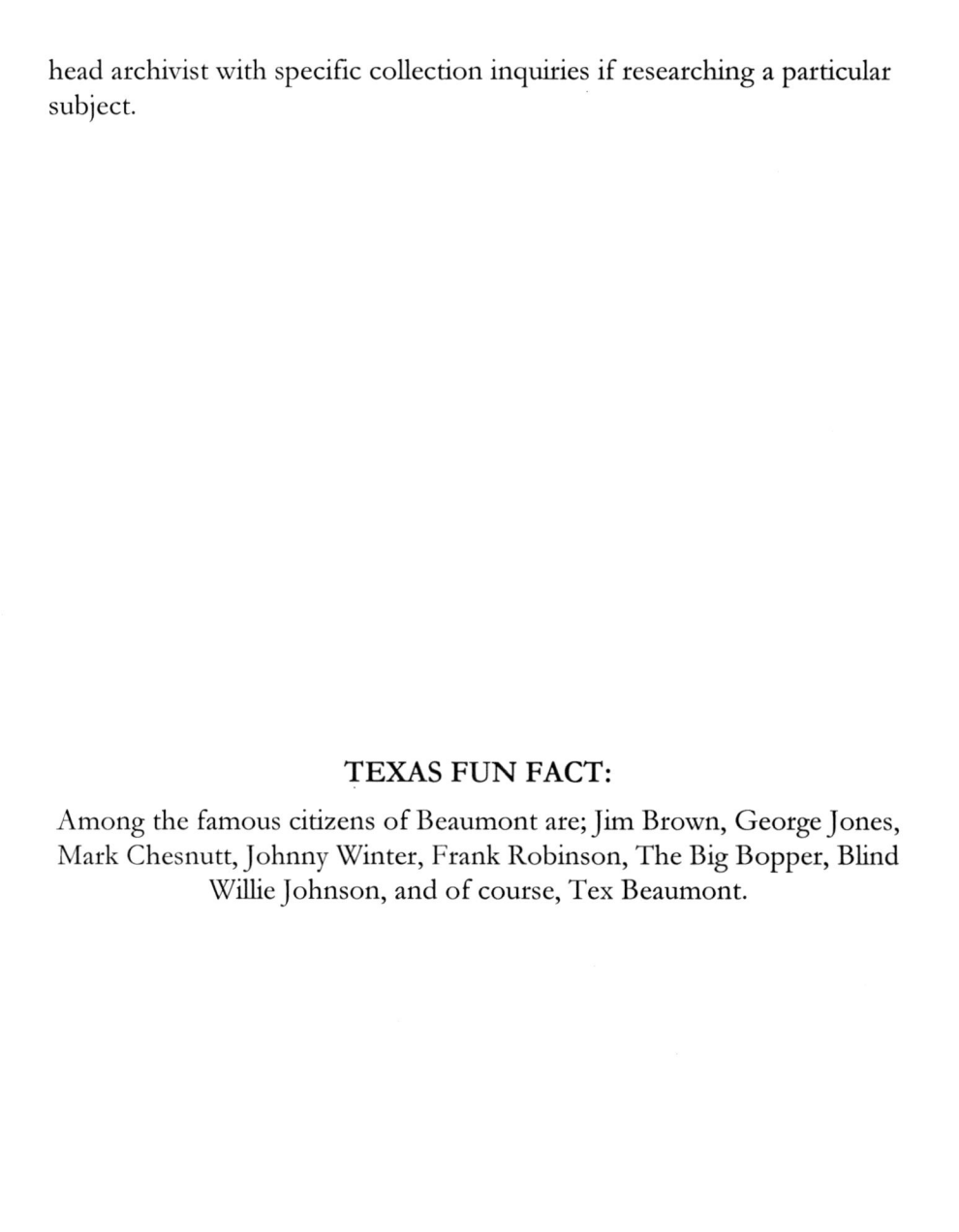

TEXAS FUN FACT:

Among the famous citizens of Beaumont are; Jim Brown, George Jones, Mark Chesnutt, Johnny Winter, Frank Robinson, The Big Bopper, Blind Willie Johnson, and of course, Tex Beaumont.

White-Pool House

112 East Murphy

Odessa, TX 79761

(432) 333-4072

www.odessahistory.com/whitpool.htm

Charles and Lucy White, along with their two sons, came to Texas in 1886. Their relocation was two-fold: Lucy's health was in need of a dryer climate, and Charles' grain business in Indiana went bankrupt in the post-Civil War era. Both reasons for the move resulted profitable for the Whites. After their arrival in Odessa, the Quaker family built a two-story red brick home in 1887 and developed the land as a farm. Charles planted the first orchards in Odessa, along with a windmill and irrigation system. He also owned a general mercantile store in town, working one of with his sons, Wilfred (who later became Postmaster and County Surveyor). As Charles' business profited, Lucy also proved the move to Texas a smart one; her health allowed her to outlive her husband, who passed away in 1905.

Lucy moved to Mineral Wells, and the three bedroom house changed hands a few times before Oso Pool purchased it in 1923. The 1927 discovery of oil in the Odessa area brought Pool to the decision to convert the home into a five unit apartment building. The switch was profitable to Pool as well, and his family owned the home until 1977 when the deed was donated to the Ector County Historical Commission. The 1887 home is now the oldest structure in Odessa, and has been restored to the original White Family plans.

Visitors to the White-Pool House can enjoy the beaded ceilings, sculpted moldings and varnished woodwork in the traditionally furnished home (complete with the wood-burning fireplaces). Two periods in the area's history are represented—ranching in the 1880's and the 1920's oil boom. The home is on the National Register of Historical Homes, and contains a small museum with regularly changing exhibits. An on-site barn replica adds to the early ranching life exhibit, and the windmill and 14-foot red sandstone water cistern adds to the charm.

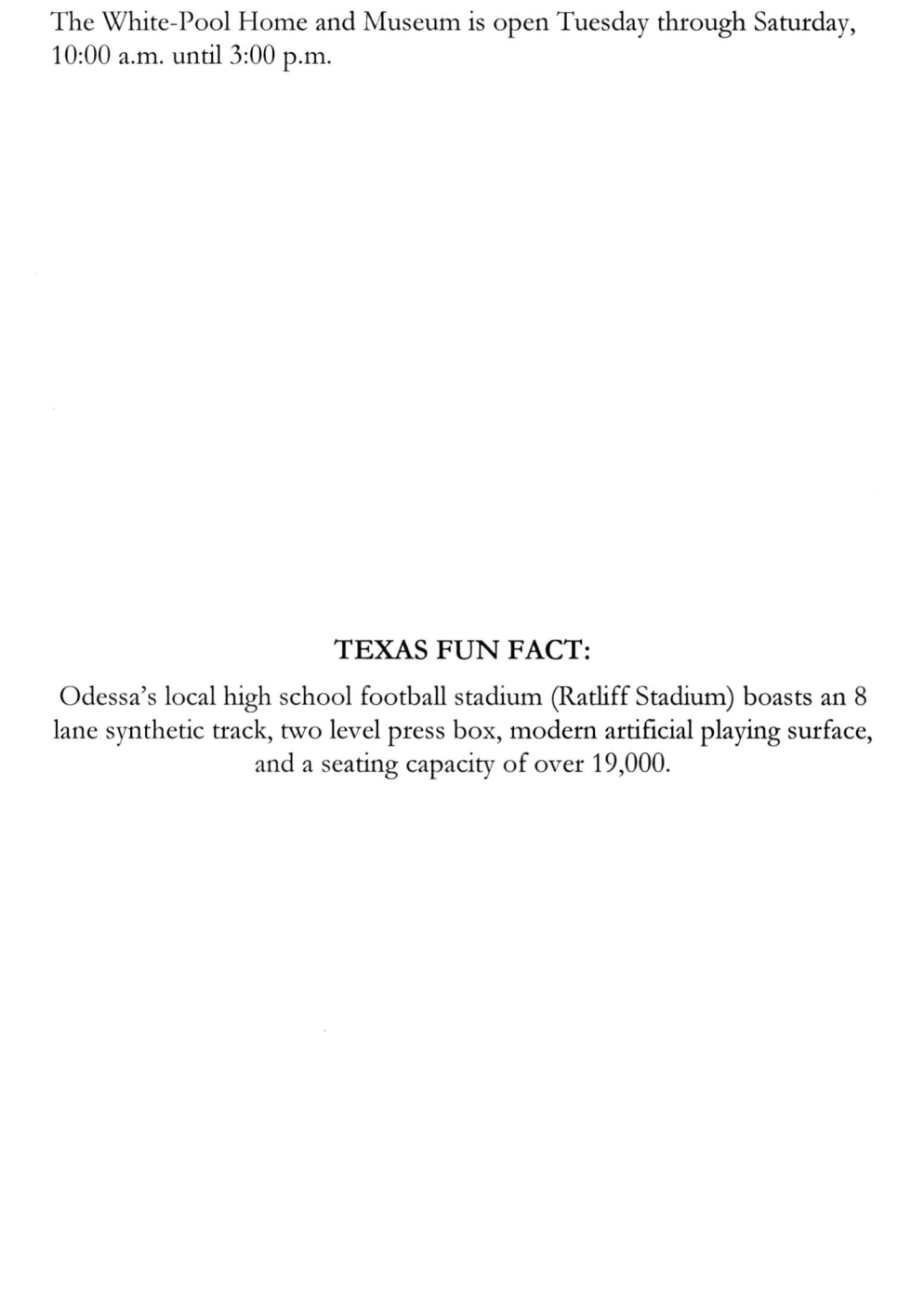

The White-Pool Home and Museum is open Tuesday through Saturday, 10:00 a.m. until 3:00 p.m.

TEXAS FUN FACT:

Odessa's local high school football stadium (Ratliff Stadium) boasts an 8 lane synthetic track, two level press box, modern artificial playing surface, and a seating capacity of over 19,000.

HISTORY MUSEUMS

Bell County Museum

201 N. Main

Belton, TX 76513

(254) 933-5243

www.bellcountytx.com/Museum

On the corner of First and Main streets in downtown Belton, visitors will find the Bell County Museum. However, BCM is not the average-everyday historical museum, but an interactive wealth of information about the county's past and people. The Beaux-Arts style Carnegie Library Building was built in 1904, and restored in 1991 as the new Bell County Museum. It is one of only twelve remaining Carnegie Libraries in Texas still in use, and sits on the Historical Chisholm Trail.

Visitors to the Bell County Museum will find information about Central Texas before Bell County's establishment in 1850 to present day (although the museum's concentration is on the first one hundred years of the county). Written and pictorial passports are available to learners of all ages and abilities to guide through the museum's timeline. Visitors have the opportunity to grind corn with the Native Americans, using a *mano* and *metate*, or with the pioneers using hand-operated machines. Stations are present to listen to a recorded pioneer message about early farm life, or discover outlaws and legends through a touch-screen computer. A cotton gin and well pump are also available, encouraging a hands-on connection with the past. A peek inside the 40-drawer "Curiosity Cabinet" will find small objects important to the time, while radio programs and videos provide other period-specific links to important events in the Central Texas area. Collections include an extensive Moustache Cup assortment, Native American Indian artifacts, and a life chronicle of Ma Ferguson, Texas' first female governor and a Bell County native. Pictures in the museum are large reproductions, clear and beautifully mounted with information about the significance posted beside each.

The Bell County Museum is open noon to 5:00 p.m., Tuesday through Saturday. In addition to the permanent exhibits, the museum also hosts temporary displays and educational workshops. Contact the Museum for details about upcoming events and exhibits, but visitors will find the permanent interactive collections worth the visit.

TEXAS FUN FACT:

Belton is home to Texas' oldest continuously published weekly newspaper *The Belton Journal*.

Border Patrol Museum

4315 Trans Mountain Rd.

El Paso, TX 79924

(915) 759-6060

www.borderpatrolmuseum.com

The United States Border Patrol was established in 1924 with the newly approved Immigration Act. The challenge of cutting off smuggling and prevention of illegal alien entry proved to be a hard job; Prohibition encouraged over-the-border bootlegging and America's reputation as the "Land of Opportunity" persuaded immigrants to find their way across the nation's borders- with or without permission. Throughout the decades, it was not uncommon to hear gunfire exchanges, both sides of the border determined to get what they wanted. However, the Border Patrol quickly earned the reputation as a fast acting, unwavering force, protecting our nation at any cost.

As "El Paso's Best Kept Secret", the Border Patrol Museum accounts the history of the institution, from the horse-and-saddle era to the days of "RAD" (Robot Against Drugs), the remote controlled robot used for drug awareness training. Although the Border Patrol's responsibility runs the perimeter of the United States, the small El Paso museum is the only one of its kind- from sea to shining sea. Happy to share stories and items from other sides of the border, the museum also holds memorabilia from all over. Included is a cigarette boat, a makeshift raft (two truck hoods welded together), bicycles, confiscated weapons and numerous articles, photographs and stories about creative plans to sneak past the Patrol Officers (one fellow tied cow hooves to his feet to change the footprints).

The Border Patrol Museum also displays names of officers killed on duty. Visitors may sit and read about each officer in a book compiled by the museum. The "Lady Liberty" exhibit shares diaries and experiences of immigration from the immigrants' viewpoint. Deeply interesting, the museum will take some time for thought. The items and artifacts are appealing and novel, however the lifeblood of the museum lies in the reading of the informational text throughout.

The Border Patrol Museum is open 9:00 a.m. until 5:00 p.m. Tuesday through Saturday and closed major holidays. Guided tours are available, but please call ahead to make sure nothing else is scheduled, as they are minimally staffed.

Within a short walking distance of the Border Patrol Museum is the El Paso Museum of Archaeology. This museum tells the story of ancient inhabitants of the area through dioramas and artifacts. Call (915) 755-4332 or go to www.elpasotexas.gov/archmuseum for details.

TEXAS FUN FACT:

El Paso is closer to the California Border than it is to Dallas.

Central Texas Area Museum

1 Main Street (P.O. Box 36)

Salado, TX 76571

(254) 947-5232

http://www.ctam-salado.org

Close to the creek that bears the town's name, the Central Texas Area Museum may appear minute, but it proves itself rich with the history of Central Texas. Opened in 1959, it has been a virtual springboard for a journey into the village of Salado's history.

Visitors to the CTAM observe artifacts from the different periods of Central Texas' history. Salado Creek, the first recorded Natural Landmark in Texas, has been an integral part of each stage of the village's eras. Tonkawa Indians camped by the creek, meeting at Tablerock, a large limestone monolith on the creek bank. Scottish colonizer Sterling Robertson from Tennessee brought settlers to Salado as part of Mexico's attempt to lay claim to Texas. The young community also met here in the late 1800's, but a great flood in 1921 caused the rock to tilt, then later crack. The remains of Tablerock are across the creek from the current Pace Park, but listening to the local stories will bring memories of a time before the breaks.

Chisholm Trail and stagecoach travelers found Salado as a welcome water stop. Salado Creek is spring-fed from the Edward's Aquifer- the only major water supply in Texas that requires no advance treatment. Ruts made by the stagecoaches of the time remain in the creek bed on the north side of the creek. During the Civil War, many famous visitors fancied a stop in Salado- including General George Custer, Captain Robert E. Lee (the General's son), cattle baron Shanghai Pierce, and outlaws Jesse James and Sam Bass. Sam Houston also frequented, once making a speech from the local inn, urging Texas to not secede from the union. The museum has varied hours, provides classes and sponsors events throughout the year, including the Scottish Clan Gathering and Highland Games in November. Call for details.

Central Texas Oil Patch Museum

421 E. Davis

Luling, TX 78648

(830) 875-1922

www.oilmuseum.org

Luling was established in 1874 at the intersection of the Galveston, Harrisburg and San Antonio railroad lines. The humble commercial beginnings of this town started with cattle, and later the citizens found a considerable profit in cotton. This profit, however, would prove miniscule later in 1922. On August 9, Edgar B. Davis discovered an oil field twelve miles long and two miles wide. Nearly overnight, the little town of Luling went from a population of 500 to 5,000. By 1924, Luling produced 11 million barrels of oil per year.

Today, the Central Texas Oil Patch Museum strives to sustain the history of what put Luling's name on the map. The museum was founded in 1990 and holds the oil business treasures in the historical Walker Brothers Building—a former credit mercantile operation. Visitors can view a timeline, maps, various tools of the trade, and oil company memorabilia, including a 1930's "Magnolia Gasoline" gas pump and decals, patches, toys, and clothing. The hard hat collection includes an intricately ornamented cover from Indonesia.

Tourists can sit in the "Oil Tank Theater" (yes, made from a real oil tank) and watch a 22-minute film about the oil business in the Central Texas area, or chat with locals about memories and stories about the town or the deeds and philanthropic acts Edgar B. Davis did with his oil money.

The Central Texas Oil Patch Museum is open Monday through Friday, 9:00 a.m. to noon and 1:00 p.m. until 5:00 p.m., and Saturdays from 10:00 a.m. until 4:00 p.m. The Chamber of Commerce is next door, and has information about Luling's numerous annual festivals and the Zedler Mill Paddling Trail. The Paddling Trail is on six miles of the San Marcos River, and is free for those with canoes and transportation.

Deaf Smith County Museum

400 Sampson

Hereford, TX 79045

(806) 363-7070

www.deafsmithcountymuseum.org

Erastus "Deaf" Smith, hero of San Jacinto and the most trusted soldier in Sam Houston's army, never set foot in the county that bears his name. However, this former Captain of the Texas Rangers is honored as this county's namesake for his integral part in forming our beloved state. It was Smith who literally "cut off" the Mexican army's main retreat at San Jacinto by destroying Vince's Bridge prior to the battle with an axe, helping guide the Texans to victory.

While the museum does not honor Deaf Smith per se, it pays homage to early settlers in the area. In the early 1880's, the western half of Deaf County belonged to the XIT Ranch. After railways and the state road system came to Deaf Smith County, as well as the discovery of the Ogallala Aquifer, the area grew into and remains one of the largest cattle feeding centers in Texas.

The Deaf Smith County Museum is a collection of items that shows "How Our Pioneers Lived, Worked, and Played". Early Native American items include arrow points, pottery and tools. The country store shows how the store not only was a resource for necessary provisions, but a social center as well. Displays of various keepsakes from the first churches in the county fill the chapel with the reminder of the importance of faith in the lives of the early settlers. Information about the World War II Prisoner Camp, Hereford Internment Area, is also shared as an integral part of the community's past.

Outdoors, visitors will enjoy a replica of one of the first homes in the area. Since the land did not provide trees or stones for shelters to be built up, the pioneers "dug in", somehow knowing that the future would bring great things. A Santa Fe caboose and historic windmill are popular photo opportunities for visitors.

Nearby, visitors will also find the E. B. Black House, a Victorian home registered as a Texas Historical Landmark. The grounds include a gazebo and beautiful flower garden—yet another opportunity to connect with the past through photography. The house is available for private parties and receptions as well as group meetings.

The museum is open Monday through Friday, 10:00 a.m. until noon and 1:00 p.m. to 5:00 p.m., and Saturdays 10:00 a.m. to noon and 1:00 p.m. until 3:00 p.m. Visitors can contact the museum office to arrange a tour for the E. B. Black House, which is also free of charge.

TEXAS FUN FACT:

The Texas City Disaster in 1947 happened when the French S.S. Grandcamp exploded while docked in Texas City. With wartime explosive chemicals on board, a fire started. During the attempts to extinguish it, the ship exploded, along with numerous nearby companies and storage facilities. The 576 known death count and extensive damage brought new laws to chemical transportation.

Fire Museum of Texas
400 Walnut
Beaumont, TX 77704
(409) 880-3927
www.firemuseumoftexas.org

Beaumont's Fire Museum of Texas has its mind on kids. Their deep-rooted mission of fire safety and history education extends out from the building to the street. Visitors of all ages first notice the enormous fire hydrant, humorously spotted with traditional Dalmatian black-on-white. Similarly painted smaller hydrants line the walkways of the museum's front garden, inviting guests to step in and enjoy a time of learning.

Hands-on activities top the style at the FMT, as children (and willing adults) try on turnout gear, climb around a fire truck, and explore safety equipment. The Fire Safety Activity Center also boasts a child-sized, two-story safety house to practice fire drills and other safety practices. Although the Activity Center and outside fire hydrant are the popular attractions for most, the historical commitment of the museum is quite apparent.

The Fire Museum of Texas is home to eleven fire vehicles, dating from 1856 to present, including a horse drawn fire wagon. A 1931 Light Truck with its original front cab is also part of the collection; this truck responded to the emergencies of the New London School Explosion in 1937 (180 miles away) and the Texas City Disaster in 1947 (98 miles away). A 1779 Chinese hand pump and a hand-drawn tub pumper from 1856 top the extensive collection of equipment the museum shares with guests. "Famous Fire" information, photographs, patches, and other memorabilia share the history of firefighting. And yes, Virginia, there is a fire pole.

The Fire Museum of Texas is housed in the 1927 Beaumont Fire Department Headquarters. In 1984, the building was designated as a Texas Historical Landmark, and 1986 brought the Texas State Fireman and Fire Marshall's Association endorsement as the "official fire museum of Texas." The museum is open from 8:00 a.m. until 4:30 p.m., Monday through Friday, and is closed major holidays. The giant hydrant, however, is always available for photographs.

TEXAS FUN FACT:

The Fire Museum of Texas' giant hydrant was created in Disney Land, California in 1999 to promote the video release of *101 Dalmatians*. The working (via the top sprinkler) hydrant stands 24'2" and weighs 4,500 pounds. While it is not the World's Largest Hydrant, it is the World's Largest *Working* Hydrant (the largest is a 4-story sculpture in Columbia, South Carolina)

TEXAS FUN FACT:

The New London School Explosion was a natural gas accident that killed 298 students and teachers in March of 1937. The explosion led to the state odorization law, requiring a distinct smell be added to natural gas, warning of its presence. A memorial was erected in 1939, sculpted by the author's distant cousin, Herring Coe.

George Washington Carver Museum and Cultural Center

1165 Angelina St.

Austin, TX 78702

(512) 974-4926

http://www.ci.austin.tx.us/carver

The George Washington Carver Museum and Cultural Center is steeped in firsts. Its beginnings as Austin's first library in 1926 grew into another first. When the collection outgrew the 1,896 square foot building, a new main library was built in 1933. The original building was moved to Angelina Street and became Austin's first library *branch*. The building was named George Washington Carver Branch Library in 1947. Yet again, growth necessitated a larger facility, so a new Carver Library was built in 1979, and the old building was dedicated in 1980 as a black history museum. There had been no other neighborhood museums dedicated to African American history in Texas—Carver was again, the first.

Today, the George Washington Carver Museum and Cultural Center has over 36,000 square feet of museum space, allocated towards four exhibit areas, a 134-seat theatre, dance studio, dark room, and much more. The pride of achieving so many "firsts" in earlier days carries over to today. The Carver gladly shares temporary and permanent exhibits with visitors. The Juneteenth Gallery shows the history and celebrations of the holiday. The Family Gallery features ten families integral to Central Texas, and the Children's Museum, *Let's Pretend, Dr. Carver!* provides a hands-on approach to learning about African American scientists and inventors. The museum's goal of providing positive role models for all children (and adults) shines through the various museum programs: art, storytelling, author and artist visits, teen photography classes, movie presentations and live music performances. A select few of the programs may require a ticket purchase, but most events and activities are free of charge. Check the website or call for specifics.

The George Washington Carver Museum and Cultural Center is open Monday, Wednesday and Friday, 9:30 am to 6:00 p.m., Tuesday and Thursday 9:30 a.m. to 8:00 p.m., and Saturday 1:00 p.m. until 5:00 p.m.

The museum is closed on Sundays. Adjacent to the Carver is Kealing Park, open 5:00 a.m. to 10:00 p.m. daily. There is a softball park, tennis courts, a playground, picnic tables, and a pavilion for public use on the twenty acre park.

TEXAS FUN FACT:

Union general Gordon Granger read the Emancipation Proclamation on June 19, 1865, in Galveston on the corner of 22nd and Strand, freeing over 250,000 slaves in Texas.

Hutchinson County Historical Museum

618 N. Main St.

Borger, TX 79007

(806) 273-0130

www.hutchinsoncountymuseum.org

Hutchinson County is best known for the Adobe Walls battles. Fort Adobe was set up in 1843 as a Comanche-Kiowa trading post, and remained until 1848 when increased dissension forced abandonment. The Native American tribes took over the fort, and increasingly continued attacks on wagon trains "trespassing" through their territory. In 1864, Col. Christopher "Kit" Carson was charged with leading the expedition to invade the former Anglo trading post. He led the attack, and then burned the village, killing the Kiowa-Apache chief Iron Shirt, who refused to leave his teepee. Kit Carson called retreat after earning a victory over the numerous Native Americans. Ten years later, a second Battle of Adobe Walls took place, again a dispute over territory that ended in Anglo victory.

During the county's early stages, the cattle industry proved viable, as well as wheat and sorghum production. The Oil Boom hit in 1926, declaring Borger (then seat of county) one of the rowdiest oil boom towns of the year. Things died down with the Depression and the county's proximity to the Dust Bowl, and although population eventually picked back up with wheat farming, the area did not return to its size before the devastation hit. Today, the Hutchinson County visitors come primarily for tourism to Lake Meredith National Recreation Area and Alibates National Monument. Petroleum products and manufacturing of oil equipment continue to provide livelihood for Hutchinson County residents.

The Hutchinson County Museum is found in Borger, although Stinnett is the current county seat. The museum is in the 1927 Grand Hotel/Hardware Building built by Greek immigrant brothers Gus and John Yiantsou. The museum, dedicated in 1977, displays the extent of

Hutchinson County's history—"Our country from war bonnets to hard hats"—as stated upstairs in the former hotel. Numerous artifacts from Adobe Walls, Native American cultures, early pioneers, ranching, oil industry work, and other eras are proudly shared. Items of particular interest include a Kiowa war bonnet that once belonged to Chief Dohasan Little Mountain, who led members of his tribe to the battle in 1864. A Boy Scouts of America exhibit contains uniforms, tools, and reference material from the early 1900's. At the top of the stairs, a life sized painting if Quanah Parker meets visitors, welcoming a tour in and around the many rooms of numerous items, respectfully displayed and labeled.

The Hutchinson County Museum staff is pleasant and willing to answer questions or provide information about any of the exhibits. The museum is quite involved with the community, and provides programs and living history talks, as well as temporary exhibits to meet the needs and interests of the people they serve. The museum is open 9:00 a.m. to 5:00 p.m., Monday through Friday, and 11:00 a.m. to 4:30 p.m. on Saturday. They are closed Sunday and holidays. The city of Borger has recently applied, through the Texas Historical Commission, for the Main Street City Program. They look forward to acceptance as Main Street businesses work to restore and improve storefront façades.

TEXAS FUN FACT:

In its early days, Borger was referred to as "Booger Town" due to the fact that many criminals and outlaws moved into town to take advantage of the "oil rush".

Llano County Museum

310 Bessemer

Llano, TX

(325) 247-3026

www.llanochamber.org

Northbound on Highway 16, just after crossing the Roy B. Inks Bridge, an 800 foot four-span riveted Parker steel truss, visitors will find the Llano County Museum. The museum is in the old Bruhl Drugstore built in 1922. Visitors find various artifacts from the area, including those from area Indians and early Texan settlers. There is also a small polo exhibit, as Llano boasts itself as the hometown to Cecil Smith, a worldwide known polo player.

The museum grounds are also home to a restored log cabin with humble furnishings, a bell, and a historical marker for the Bruhl Drugstore. Various 1900's era buildings sprinkle the area as well, including grocery stores, historic homes, and the 1910 Cassaday-Grey Granite Co. building. Although the iron deposits in the area put Llano on the map, the granite industry, along with ranching and farming, has sustained Llano throughout the years. The Llano Uplift, granite domes and outcrops throughout the county fostered the million-dollar industry, and the town pays homage to the rock, having created many of the historical markers from Texas Pink granite. The most famous outcrop is Enchanted Rock, a pink granite dome, covering 640 acres at the state historical site nearby. (There is a fee for visiting this state park). Llanite, a rare, brown granite with sky blue crystals and pink feldspar, is named for the County. Llano is the only known source of llanite.

The Llano River roars by, and visitors also enjoy Llano's historic downtown square. The Llano County Courthouse Historic District is part of the National Register of Historic Places, known for the courthouse itself, the Southern Hotel, the Badu Building, and the Llano County Jail, affectionately referred to as "Red Top". Past lawbreakers rarely spent a night in jail, but rather "stayed over at the Red Top".

Historic walking tour and historical marker maps are available at the museum and the Llano Chamber of Commerce (700 Bessemer). The museum is open 10:00 a.m. to noon and 1:30 p.m. until 5:30 p.m., Tuesday through Sunday in the summer (June-Aug), and Thursday through Sunday the rest of the year.

TEXAS FUN FACT:

The word llano is Spanish for "plain".

National Ranching Heritage Center

3121 Fourth Street

Lubbock, TX 79409-3200

(806) 742-0498

www.ttu.edu/RanchingHeritageCenter

Under the direction of Texas Tech University, the National Ranching Heritage Center strives to provide insight and appreciation for the area's early pioneers and ranchers. Since its dedication in July 1976, the NRHC has grown to encompass 46 authentic structures representing Texas Panhandle life from the 1700's until the early 1900's.

Upon arrival, visitors are greeted by the J.J. Gibson Memorial Park. Fourteen life-sized bronze longhorns encircle the walking path, each representative of a different area ranch. While walking the trail, keep eyes peeled for area wildlife! A group of jackrabbits is known to call this place home along with the bronzed cattle.

The center's inside exhibits range from period artifacts coupled with interactive items to artistic renditions of ranch life, sparking not only an understanding, but an appreciation for the way of life. While the exhibits change regularly, information and photos of some past shows are available online. The website also shares podcasts about the exhibits, given by artists or other involved parties.

On the way through the back door, visitors can grab a walking tour brochure—a Heritage Center map with labels, descriptions and significance of each of the outside structures. Examples of a "dog-trot" house, half dug-out, barns, windmills, and homes wind around the outside trails. Summer visitors may enjoy witnessing children learn through educational day camp activities; students play with early pioneer toys, weave on a loom, hear about and touch area "critters", create leatherworking project, and more (there is a registration fee for the camp).

The National Ranching Heritage Center is a popular field trip spot for area schools. Lesson and activity plans, aligned with Texas educational standards, are available online for all levels—Pre-K through grade 12. Group tour guidelines are also available on the NRHC website.

Texas Tech University has a number of additional educational museums in the Lubbock area. Next door to the National Ranching Heritage Center is the Museum of Texas Tech University. The MoTTU houses a collection of artistic, cultural, and historical items specific to the Lubbock. Dinosaur skeleton replicas represent animals found in area excavations while the collection of folk art ranges from functional pieces to whimsical. The "Explorium" is a hands-on, kid-friendly space where visitors can peruse through multiple drawers containing everything from minerals to animal bones, access fun reference books, or take a closer look through a video microscope. For more information, call (806) 742-2490. TTU's Lubbock Lake Landmark is few miles away, and although self-guided tours are an option, it is highly recommended to schedule a tour with LLL personnel. There is an informational pamphlet for self-guides, but mapped sites are hard to identify if not familiar with the point of interest. Call (806) 742-1116 for tour details.

TEXAS FUN FACT:

J.J. Gibson managed the Four Sixes Ranch (6666) from 1970 until 1990. Included in his ranching achievements awards are the Texas Trailblazer Award, the Foy Procter Cowman Award of Honor, and he is a member of the American Hereford Association Hall of Fame.

Old Jail Museum

414 St. Lawrence Street

Gonzales, TX 78629

(830) 672-6532

www.gonzalestexas.com/visitor/attractions.asp

Gonzales County Jail was built between 1885 and 1887. Forged and fused, this concrete and steel building came before welding, and was built to last. The jail was actively used until 1975, and has housed many prisoners including John Wesley Hardin and Gregorio Cortez.

Today, the Old Jail Museum is also home to the Gonzales Chamber of Commerce. If lucky, jail visitors may be able to speak with one of the Chamber employees, happy to share stories and information about the jail as well as the City of Gonzales. The first floor of the museum displays information about period law enforcement, office items, and objects taken from the prisoners. The fist floor also has the "dungeon" (solitary confinement) and the "women and lunatics cell".

Upstairs, two floors are divided into prisoner cells and a double floor court area. The cement walls are etched with the names of prisoners, loved ones, and causes. Centered in the court is a reproduction of the gallows used between 1855 and 1921. Gonzales County Jail was the site for six legal hangings, and the gallows were torn down in 1950. Local legend tells of Albert Howard, the last man hanged in Gonzales on March 18, 1921. Convinced of his innocence, Albert was obsessed with the County Courthouse clock tower, constantly checking and calculating how much longer he had to live. On the day of his death, he cursed the tower, saying that if he were truly innocent as he proclaimed, the 4 clocks on the tower would never show the same time again. The clocks have not been synchronized since that day.

The Old Jail Museum is located on Courthouse Square in the middle of town. The recently renovated County Courthouse is behind the museum and the 1903 Fire Station is across the street. Historic walking maps are available at the Chamber of Commerce (inside the Old Jail Museum). The Museum is open Monday through Friday, 8:00 a.m. until 5:00 p.m., Saturday 9:00 a.m. to 4:00 p.m., and Sunday 1:00 p.m. until 4:00 p.m.

TEXAS FUN FACT:

Parts of the movie, "The Ballad of Gregorio Cortez," were filmed on location in Gonzales.

Old Nacogdoches University Building

515 North Mound Street

Nacogdoches, TX 75962

(936) 564-7351

www.cets.sfasu.edu/VR/pages/oldu.htm

Nacogdoches University was founded in 1845 under a charter granted by the Republic of Texas, as the only secular university established during this time period in our history. The university was housed in a number of temporary buildings until 1859, when the present modified Grecian structure, designed by James H. Cato, was complete.

The building has been used for educational purposed since its charter, save for two years during the end and post-Civil War. During this war, the establishment became a recuperation hospital and housing unit for Confederate soldiers, while afterwards it was the headquarters for Federal troops in Nacogdoches. After this time, only two years after its official opening in the building, the University was leased out to pay off debts and teacher back salaries. In 1870, the building was leased to a string of owners who continued the educational beginnings: the Catholic Church, the Masonic Lodge, and Louisiana's Keachi College. At this point, in 1904, the University's charter was not renewed. Some of the property was sold, and the University Building itself was deeded to the Nacogdoches School District.

Today, the "Mother of Education in Texas" is sponsored by the Center for East Texas Studies, but the building is still owned by the school district. Volunteers of the Federation of Women's Clubs provide docents to share stories of the oldest town in Texas. Area history and artifacts are displayed, including desks used in the early formal educational days of the building (found upstairs). Downstairs, elegant period furniture is displayed, including twin mirrors said to have been smuggled from the home of Mexico's last emperor and empress, Maximilian and his wife, Carlota.

Another fun piece in the museum is the Nacogdoches Opera House piano. As the story goes, the Marx Brothers, in their humble beginnings, started as a musical act. In 1912, they performed as *The Six Mascots* in downtown Nacogdoches, playing this particular piano. Shouts of a runaway mule interrupted their performance, as audience members ran outside to watch the action. Upon their return, the upset Groucho made the snide remarks, "Nacogdoches is full of roaches" and "The jackass is the flower of Tex-ass." Much to his surprise, the angry comments roused laughter; the performers continued with the insulting jokes, and *The Marx Brothers* comedy act was born. There is also a hand written letter from Groucho, thanking the mayor for accepting him as an honorary citizen of Nacogdoches.

The Old Nacogdoches University Building is open daily except Monday, from 1:00 p.m. to 4:00 p.m., and is closed major holidays. While in the area, tourists can enjoy other architectural and historical attractions. Most buildings, regardless of age, are privately owned, with a few exceptions. Driving tour maps are available at the Nacogdoches Visitor Center located at 200 East Main (www.visitnacogdoches.org).

TEXAS FUN FACT:

The Old Nacogdoches University bell came from Whitechapel Bell Foundry, creators of America's Liberty Bell in Pennsylvania, and London's Westminster Abbey bells, and Great Bell ("Big Ben").

TEXAS FUN FACT:

Freedonia, the country portrayed in The Marx Brother's movie, "Duck Soup", shares a name (although spelled differently) with Gregg County Fredonia, a Texas town 60 miles north of Nacogdoches. (There is also a Fredonia in Mason County, 315 miles east of Nacogdoches.)

Smith County Museum

125 South College

Tyler, TX 75702

(903) 592-5993

www.smithcountyhistory.org

Early records of Smith County evidence the area as populated by Caddo Indians centuries before European visitors to the land. The Caddo tribe relocated in the late 18th century, making way for Cherokee, led by Chief Bowles. The area occupation further slowed Anglo settlement, but it did not stop. The effects of the 1839 Cherokee War removed the tribe from the county, and new settlers found their way to East Texas.

Tyler's traditional climate of frequent, warm rains, along with the rich soil made the new Anglo pioneers understand why the land was inhabited by the agricultural Caddo for so long. The land provided for quick and rich agricultural growth—fruit and roses in particular. These contributed to the increased economy of early Texas, and Smith County became an economic center. With money comes power, and the county became a political center as well; first of the Republic of Texas, and later in statehood.

Military influence has also been prevalent in Smith County. Camp Ford, near Tyler, served as a POW camp during the Civil War, while Camp Fannin (about ten miles north of Tyler) served as an infantry training center during World War II.

The Smith County Museum is housed in the historic 1904 Andrew Carnegie Library Building, and is run by the Smith County Historical Society. Utilized as a library until 1980, the building now shares Smith County's history from the Caddo Indians, through settlement, economic and political development as well as "recent" history from the past 100 years. Downstairs hosts a timeline of exhibits, as well as an Archives and Research facility; upstairs, various historical films are shown in the Payne

Auditorium. The auditorium also provides a popular spot for public meetings.

The Smith County Historical Society members volunteer as docents at the museum, and prove to be quite knowledgeable about the area's history, fun facts, and local anecdotes. It is easy to loose track of time while learning about the county quirks and inside stories. The Smith County Museum is open Monday through Friday from 10:00 a.m. until 4:00 p.m., and guided tours are provided on demand (although they appreciate a nice "please"). If planning a large group visit, please call ahead; the Society will happily arrange additional guides. The Smith County Historical Society also cares for Camp Ford, the largest Civil War Prisoner camp west of the Mississippi. Camp Ford is located off of State highway 271, north of Tyler. Call or see SCHS website for details.

While in Tyler, visitors enjoy the Main Street District, participant of the Texas Historical Commission's Main Street Program, accredited by the National Main Street Program (www.heartoftyler.com).

TEXAS FUN FACT:
Amazingly, Tyler Texas has seven official web-sites.

Texas Surf Museum

309-A North Water Street

Corpus Christi, TX 78401

(361) 888-7873

www.texassurfmuseum.com

Corpus Christi is the proud home to Texas' one and only surf museum. Found in the Water Street District, Texas Surf Museum strives to prove that "Texas is not just the land of cowboys and oil barons," but of coastal surfers, as well. They do it, too, through displays of surfboards and memorabilia from area lovers of the sport. Visitors need not be surfers themselves to enjoy the museum; the staff does an incredible job of providing written explanations of each artifact, including product specifics and personal histories.

The temporary exhibits change yearly, but permanent displays include a projections theatre with a continuous show of local surfing footage or period beach movies, a board shaping garage and the Texas Gulf Coast Mural—a mesh of map and surfer photos (historical and current) that shows the entire coast of Texas. Outside, a concrete, life-sized Ford woody notes the museum's entrance, over which hangs a Texas flag-designed surfboard. Art boards, movie and sports posters, clothing, surfboards and other equipment centered on the yearly theme shape the temporary exhibits that change each June.

Attached to the front of the Texas Surf Museum is Surf Club Records, sponsor of the South Texas Music Walk of Fame. Numerous recording artists from Southern Texas are memorialized within the stars of the walk, including Freddie Martinez, Sr., Michael Nesmith, Kris Kristopherson, Selena and Freddie Fender. The South Texas Music Walk of Fame is always accessible, and the Texas Surf Museum is open daily: Monday through Wednesday, 10:00 a.m. to 7:00 p.m., Thursday through Saturday, 10:00 a.m. until 10:00 p.m., and Sunday 11:00a.m. until 5:00 p.m.

Wharton County Museum

3615 N. Richmond

Wharton, TX 77488

(979) 532-2600

www.whartoncountyhistoricalmuseum.com/index.html

Wharton County was originally established in 1823 as part of Stephen F. Austin's "Old Three Hundred"—first Anglo settlements in Texas sponsored by the Mexican government. After achieving independence, the area was reestablished in 1846 as Wharton County, named after two brothers who served the Republic at San Jacinto.

The Wharton County Museum was established in 1979. The community, proud its history, has come together to share in the 15,000+ square foot exhibit—a mix and mingle of all things Wharton. From farm and ranch exhibits to a room dedicated to Texasgulf Sulphur, local college history to Horton Foote and Dan Rather, this place has a little of everything. This conglomeration of cultures and history may sound like too much for one county museum to handle, but the WCM pulls it off with style.

The building that the WCM calls home is actually a two-part deal. The front is a relocated county jail, and the back half is former home to Marshall and Lillie Johnson, major benefactors of the museum. Within its walls, visitors can see an original Texas land grant for Wharton County, signed three times by Sam Houston, exhibits on the healing arts, education, churches, and the military, including native Wharton County Medal of Honor recipients Roy Benavidez (U.S. Army) and Johnnie D. Hutchins (U.S. Navy).

Another draw to the museum is Marshall Johnson's collection animal trophies from all over the world. The octagonal and adjacent "Texas" rooms are home to over 100 animals, many world-class, and some world records at the time of collection. Avid hunters stand in awe of the extent and quality of animal trophies.

The Wharton County Museum also offers a free research facility. The majority of stored information includes family, church and court records from the county, including original court books from the Republic of Texas. Numerous photographs are available as well—most are catalogued, some are not. The research facility only charges a minimal fee for copies. In the research room, take note of the fireplace. Marshall Johnson had it made using stones and crystals from his personal collection from around the world. It is a fantastic artistic addition to the museum and should not be overlooked.

The Wharton County Museum is open daily, Monday through Friday 9:30 a.m. to 4:30 p.m., and weekends from 1:00 pm. until 5:00 p.m.

TEXAS FUN FACT:

MSG Roy Benavidez is buried at Fort Sam Houston in San Antonio. The photographer, Stuart Lloyd, met him when MSG Benavidez visited Fort Hood.

Wichita Falls Railroad Museum
500 9th St.
Wichita Falls, TX 76308-0242
(940) 723-2661
www.wfrrm.com

It is said that future site of Wichita Falls was won by Mississippi native John A. Scott in a New Orleans poker game in the late 1837, and proceeded to do nothing with the land for 40 years, due to the "misplaced" land certificates. His heirs hired M.W. Seeley to map the area in 1876 after they rediscovered the lost certificates. These families, and those who were found on the land already, eventually moved onto different parts of Texas, making way for Wichita Falls' first permanent family of Barwise. Judge Joseph Barwise came to be known as the city's true founding father; it was he who brought the railroad and prosperity to the little north Texas town.

The Wichita Falls Railroad Museum was founded in 1980 as a part of the National Register of Historic Districts of downtown Wichita Falls. The museum pays homage to the institution that helped make Wichita Falls great—the railroad. The museum is located in Depot Square, the former Union Passenger Station, and has a number of items within their three-track property.

On the museum ground tracks, visitors will find a large collection of rolling stock, including an FW&D steam locomotive. Originally a coal burner in 1906, it was converted in 1929. Other cars include the "Art Train" (www.artrainusa.org), a passenger car, diesel trains, cabooses, and a 1913 Pullman Sleeper. If guests are lucky and at the museum on one of the select Saturdays, the MKT Troop Sleeper may be open—it is home to a 20' by 6' model HO-Scale railroad layout. Another museum favorite is the "Kiddie Train" provided by local business sponsors.

The Wichita Falls Railroad Museum is open from noon until 4:00 p.m., Tuesday through Saturday, but gates close at 3:30 p.m. to ensure visitors have some time to see the museum before closing. The museum is also open for area school field trips and birthday parties; however, fees are charged for both of these services.

TEXAS FUN FACT:

Not far from the Railroad Museum, "The World's Littlest Skyscraper" sits on the corner of 7th Street and LaSalle Alley. Local legend claims that the building was a part of an oil boom scam in 1919; an unnamed individual drew up plans and convinced sponsors to invest $200,000 in the much needed office space. What he didn't share, however, was that the plans were drawn in inches rather than feet. Not wanting to appear dishonest, he built the skyscraper—a whopping 10' X 16' four story building. The lower floor once housed six desks, representing six different companies—just in case the investors wanted to check the validity of the accepted proposal. The swindler's name has never been revealed, and he's not been heard from since. The building now houses an antique shop whose owner joyfully shares the building's history with anyone who asks.

UNIQUELY TEXAS

The Alamo

300 Alamo Plaza (P.O. Box 2599)

San Antonio, TX 78299

(210) 225-1391

www.thealamo.org

The Alamo was once known by the Spanish as Mission San Antonio de Valero, and throughout its three hundred year history, it has been a mission, military barracks, a fort during the Texas Revolution, and now as a monument for all that is truly Texan.

While the fact remains that Texans suffered a traumatic loss at the Battle of the Alamo, the saying "REMEMBER THE ALAMO!" became a rallying cry later, when Texans remembered a time of defeat in order to gain victory over the Mexican Army at the Battle of San Jacinto.

Today, the Alamo is in the center of San Antonio, and the museums on the old mission grounds preserve the memories of the Alamo defenders. The historic grounds are run by The Daughters of the Republic of Texas with the intent to carry on the memory of those who achieved independence for Texas.

The mission grounds have two original structures—the Shrine and Long Barrack. Both buildings include artifacts from the battle and a history of the mission. Some tokens from Texan heroes include Davy Crockett's buckskin vest, a ring that belonged to William Travis, and a famous Jim Bowie knife. Between the two buildings, visitors have the choice of spending time with the Wall of History, Alamo Gardens, or the Convento Courtyard. Each area has its own charm, from continued history of the mission, to beautifully sculpted landscaping, and actual cannons used at the battle for which the Alamo is famous. Long Barrack also houses the Clara Driscoll Theater, named after the Daughter of the Republic who saved the mission from its planned conversion into a hotel in 1905.

The Alamo is open every day, except Christmas Eve and Christmas Day. Hours of operation are Monday- Saturday, 9:00 a.m. to 5:30 p.m., and Sundays 10:00 a.m. to 5:30 p.m. During summer months, the museum extends hours until 7:00 p.m. on Friday and Saturday nights.

TEXAS FUN FACT:

The first high-rise building in the United States to have air-conditioning was built in San Antonio in 1928.

Capitol Complex

11th Street and Congress

Austin, TX 78701

(512) 463-0063

www.tspb.state.tx.us/spb/capitol/texcap.htm

On March 2, 1836, Texas declared herself independent—out from under the reign of Mexico. Between this time and 1837, the Republic of Texas held business in five temporary locations before Sam Houston permanently moved the capitol to Houston. Mirabeau Lamar, in his term as second president, moved the capitol once again in 1839, this time to the newly formed town of Austin. The 7,135 acres were purchased for $21,000, and a city plan was put in place, dedicating four city blocks to the Capitol Building property. Texas was annexed into the United States in 1845, and Austin remained the Capitol—this time, it was the Capitol of the State of Texas.

The first Capitol Building was completed in 1853; it burned in 1881, after plans for the new building were already underway. 1875 brought a surprise to America, as Texas agreed to exchange three million acres of public land in the Panhandle for the construction of the new Capitol. Exchanging public land for a service had not been heard of before. A Chicago based company (a.k.a. "Capitol Syndicate") accepted the offer and after a design competition in 1880, E.E. Meyers was named the architect. (His domed Renaissance Revival design bares a striking resemblance to the Nation's Capitol in Washington, D.C.) The State wanted construction materials to come from her natural resources, but after traditional limestone proved "unsightly" with natural discoloration, the granite quarry in present-day Marble Falls offered free Texas pink granite to the state as building material. The State accepted.

The State of Texas was about to give America another surprise as her newest child. Texas needed labor; and it needed to be cheap labor to quarry and cut the granite within the budget. State prisoners were then "hired" for the job, upsetting the union labor organizations, whose workers refused to work alongside the non-union prisoners. Skilled granite cutters were brought from Scotland to assist the workers, but their recruitment was a violation of the Contract Labor Act of 1885, further upsetting union workers. The structure was nevertheless completed by the prisoner-labored Chicago construction company. The building was topped with the zinc Goddess of Liberty and dedicated as the new State Capitol Building in 1888, on the original dedicated area from Lamar's administration. The building and its history are quite an experience.

Today, it is easy to spend a day at the Texas State Capitol Complex. Visitors are welcome to free guided tours, or may explore the Complex independently. Guided tours of the building start on the first floor at the Treasurer's Business Office, and run between 30-45 minutes. Tours are available 8:30 a.m. until 4:30 p.m., Monday through Friday, 9:30 a.m. to 3:30 p.m. on Saturday, and noon to 3:30 p.m. on Sunday. Tourists see the starred Rotunda and dome from three levels (dome itself not open to public). The House of Representatives Chamber is the largest of the toured areas, and displays an 1836 flag from the Battle of San Jacinto behind the Speaker's desk. Other rooms proudly boast extraordinary antique furnishings, but the Library houses a chair said to have been used by Santa Anna during his Texas campaigns. Visitors will also tour the Capitol's underground extensions, although most rooms are used by Capitol staff. Throughout the tour, visitors will enjoy numerous works of art, including Elisabet Ney's sculptures of Sam Houston and Stephen F. Austin, William Henry Huddle's paintings *Davy Crockett* and *Surrender of Santa Anna*, and Enrico F. Cerracchio's marble bust of Ma Ferguson. Portraits of the Presidents of the Republic and State Governors line the inside rotunda, while landscapes and important scenes from Texas history provide décor to the offices and hallways.

After touring the Capitol Building, visitors can take a trip to the Capitol Visitor's Center. Located in the old General Land Office Building, the oldest state structure built in 1857, the Capitol Visitor's Center is also home to one of twelve Texas Travel Information Centers. Here, uniformed travel counselors can help visitors plan and map out trips around the state. Back in the Capitol Visitor's Center, tourists can view the short films "Beyond the Dome" (areas of the Capitol Building not on public tour) and "XIT" (financing of the Capitol Building). Art exhibits, information about the GLO building, and a room dedicated to O. Henry are also part of the CVC. Visitors can sit at a chunky star computer kiosk and interact with the Capitol Timeline exhibit. There is a room for temporary displays as well, containing information about the state's past or highlighting a personality or area of the state. Call or check the website for current exhibits—(512) 305-8400 or www.texascapitolvisitorscenter.com. The CVC is open Monday through Saturday 9:00-5:00 and Sunday noon-5:00. The CVC website provides lesson plans and teacher guides for before, during and after visit use as well as information about free teacher workshops.

Walking Grounds brochures are available at the Treasurer's Business Office or the Capitol Visitor's Center, and visitors are welcome to tour the Capitol Grounds 7:00 a.m. to 10:00 p.m. on weekdays and 9:00 a.m. to 8:00 p.m. on the weekends. Guide services and tours are available 8:00 a.m. to 5:00 p.m. weekdays and 9:00 a.m. until 5:00 p.m. on weekends. The Capitol Complex Grounds contain a wealth of information about the history and people of the state as well. Numerous monuments, gardens, fountains, and artifacts are found within the walls. Included are the Heroes of the Alamo monument from 1891, Terry's Texas Rangers monument from 1907 and two 24 pound howitzer cannons from 1836 (Rangers monument and one of the howitzers are on front cover with Capitol Building). Visitors are welcome to picnic and drink from the artesian well fountain (reproduced from photographs and plans of the fountain on the original Capitol Grounds), or stroll through the Johnson Texas Capitol Flower Gardens (on top of the underground extensions on the south grounds).

The Capitol Complex is open daily, and although there are extended hours during legislative sessions, some areas are not accessible for tours during these times. All guided tours throughout the complex are conducted daily except on Thanksgiving, Christmas Eve, Christmas Day, New Year's Day, and Easter. The Capitol Visitors Center and Texas Travel Information Center are both closed these holidays as well.

Chamizal National Museum

800 South San Marcial St.

El Paso, TX 79905-4123

(915) 532-7273

www.nps.gov/cham

In 1864, flooding caused a radical shift in the Rio Grande River, causing it to move 800 acres into the United States territory by 1873. The United States and Mexico had formerly agreed through signed treaties that the Rio Grande would remain, at its deepest point, the boundary between the two countries. It was also agreed that the boundary would change only by gradual erosion by natural causes. Controversy arose from this sudden shift, raising boundary questions from both countries. Mexico insisted that the river moved by natural causes, while the United States was firm in stating that the change was not gradual. This disagreement persisted for almost 100 years.

In 1964, John F. Kennedy concerned himself with the importance of bringing this long term dispute to an end, and worked with Mexico's president Adolfo Lopez Mateos to ratify the treaty that brought peace and conclusion to the issue. Both countries received land, and the battle of the border had come to an amicable end. The treaty was signed January 14, 1963.

The Chamizal Memorial is on former Mexican soil, now belonging to the United States. Visitors to the Memorial can take part of a number of indoor educational activities or walk the 1.8 mile Cordova Island Trail that encompasses the 55 acre park. Many photographic opportunities are available, as the park has views of the downtown El Paso skyline, and the Franklin and Juarez Mountains. Some picnic areas with grills are available, but the Chamizal Memorial is a popular spot, so the tables occupy quickly (no reservations- first come, first serve only). The mural on the Memorial building by Carlos Flores depicts the culture and important figures that came together for the Chamizal Agreement.

Inside, the National Parks Service provides educational opportunities for all ages. There is a self guided Junior Ranger Program booklet for children ages 6-11 available and an "Armchair Explorer Series" offers visits to other National Park sites via video every third Wednesday of the month at 10:30 a.m. and noon. Three art galleries emphasize the friendly relations between the United States and Mexico with traveling exhibits. Free Ranger-guided tours are on Tuesdays and Thursdays at 10:00 a.m., and share the story of the 100-year boundary dispute, with historical events dating back to 1848. The memorial also provides Music Under the Stars concerts and Family Days. Both are provided free of charge. Online, printable games and puzzles about the history of Chamizal are available for children.

The park grounds are open daily 5:00 a.m. until 10:00 p.m. and the Memorial Visitor Center and Museum are open Tuesday through Saturday, 10:00 a.m. until 5:00 p.m. The Chamizal Memorial is closed New Year's Day, Thanksgiving, and Christmas Day.

TEXAS FUN FACT:

The National Parks Service also hosts Web Rangers, an online informational program for "kids of all ages" to learn about different National Parks, Monuments and Historical Sites. Games and activities center around American history and difficulty level can be set to easy, medium or hard. This program is separate from the Junior Ranger booklets available at NPS sites.

Goliad's Historic Downtown Square

c/o Chamber of Commerce

231 S. Market Street

Goliad, TX 77963

(361) 645-3563 (800) 848-8674

www.goliadcc.org

"Remember the Alamo, Remember Goliad!" The San Jacinto battle cry commemorates the early Texas Revolutionary War, but Goliad is noted as one of the oldest municipalities of Texas. With its mission beginnings in 1749, the town was first referred to as Santa Dorotea. The Mission Espiritu Santo and Presidio La Bahia served the Native American tribes for 110 years. After Mexico's independence from Spain in 1829, the name changed to Goliad. Named for a Mexican Revolutionary hero, the town ironically would come to be known as the site of the bloodiest massacre in Texas' fight for independence from Mexico.

On October 9, 1835, colonists under the leadership of Ben Milam and George Collinsworth captured the Presido; 92 signatures were listed on Texas' first Declaration of Independence—all pledging dedication against the tyranny of Mexican General Antonio Lopez de Santa Anna. It is here that the first flag of Texas was flown—the "Bloody Arm Flag"—symbolizing willingness to sacrifice for the sake of freedom. By 1836, Col. James Fannin was in command of the fort, and on March 19, the site began evacuation to Victoria on General Sam Houston's orders. Before they made it to Coleto Creek, the Mexican army, under command of General Urrea, attacked the Texians. Fannin readied defenses, and fought until sundown, but the lack of water and ability to make fire that night made treating the wounded a virtual impossibility. Lack of food and ammunition left the Texians unprepared for battle the next morning. In the face of Urrea's rested, fed, armed and newly reinforced troops, Fannin surrendered, hoping for treatment and care for his troops as prisoners of war. Fannin's conditional surrender was not accepted, and the men were imprisoned in the presidio for a week before Palm Sunday, when they were marched outside and shot. Including Col. Fannin, 342 men died that day.

Goliad legend tells of Francisca Panchita Alvarez, wife of a Mexican officer. She came to be known as the "Angel of Goliad" as she begged her husband to spare the lives of Fannin's men. Her efforts saved 28 men, and her story of compassion lives on in our history.

This story of the Goliad Massacre, and many more, are immortalized within various memorial sites in and around the city. Goliad's Courthouse Square Historic District contains buildings, memorials and trees from the times of the stories. The Goliad Chamber of Commerce provides a walking tour map of the significant places interest, including Fannin Plaza Park, the Market House Museum and the Hanging Tree from the 1857 Cart War. The Chamber also provides a hike/bike trail map named in honor of the Angel of Goliad. The two mile trail is lined with native plants and trees, all described in the informational pamphlet. The trail follows the San Antonio River, and leads to the burial site and memorial of Col. Fannin and men.

The Goliad Chamber of Commerce is open 8:00 a.m. to noon and 1:00 p.m. to 5:00 p.m., Monday through Friday. On the second Saturday of each month, they are open from 6:30 a.m. until 11:30 a.m. to support the town's "Market Days." Chamber employees welcome visitors and gladly share information and answer questions about the town's history and various attractions.

TEXAS FUN FACT:

Goliad is a phonetic anagram of Hidalgo ("h" is silent in Spanish pronunciation). Father Miguel Hidalgo y Costilla is a Mexican Revolutionary hero.

Gonzalez Memorial Museum

414 Smith St.

Gonzales, TX 78629

(830) 672-6350

www.cityofgonzales.org/museum

Gonzales was established in 1825 by Empresario Green DeWitt and by 1933, it was the capitol of the DeWitt colony. In 1831, the Mexican government provided Gonzales with a six-pound cannon as protection against the increasing Indian attacks. However, by 1835, the Mexican government demanded the return of the cannon as conflicts rose between Texas and Mexico, and sent six soldiers and an oxcart to retrieve it. The cannon was not returned, but was instead buried in a nearby peach orchard. The Mexican Army later returned to the river with over 100 mounted men, determined to take the cannon. Eighteen—later known as "The Old Eighteen"—stood their ground and held off the Mexicans by hiding the ferry, waiting for assistance to arrive. As Texan forces grew, women volunteers fashioned a flag, sporting an image of the cannon and the phrase "Come and Take It". On October 2, 1835, the Texans crossed the river and challenged the Mexican soldiers, shooting off the cannon. "The Shot Heard 'Round the World" was Texas' first action in the fight for independence from Mexico. The surprised Mexican army quickly retreated as the Texas Revolution was on its way.

The cannon that symbolizes Texas' thirst for freedom now finds a home, not buried in a peach orchard, but as the central attraction in the Gonzales Memorial Museum. In 1936 the museum opened as a commemorative building for Texas' Centennial celebration. Made of Texas shell stone, the building hosts two wings, one dedicated to the early history of Gonzales and the Texas Revolution, the other showcases memorabilia from the town's people since the pioneer age. The historical wing with the cannon also has a number of documents and photographs, as well as an 1892 United Confederate flag. The south wing featuring the people of the area has clothing, accessories, dolls, toys, dishes, cameras, and a variety of other paraphernalia from Gonzales families through the years.

The museum grounds also has a bronze plaque dedicated to the "Old Eighteen" and a pink granite memorial for the "Immortal Thirty-two", men from Gonzales who fought and died in the battle of the Alamo. An amphitheatre finishes the building's backside, and has been used for many area events in the past. Although not used often presently, it is still a sight to enjoy while on the grounds.

The Gonzales Memorial Museum is open 10:00 a.m. to noon and 1:00 p.m. to 5:00 p.m. Tuesday through Saturday, and 1:00 p.m. until 5:00 p.m. Sundays. Visitors can also see the "Come and Take It" battleground, approximately seven miles southwest of Gonzales Hwy. 97 on Spur 95. The city also hosts the "Come and Take It" Festival the first weekend in October annually with no grounds fees for limited events.

TEXAS FUN FACT:

Texas was an independent nation from 1836 to 1845.

Hall of State

3939 Grand Avenue

Dallas, TX 75210

(214) 421-4500

www.hallofstate.com

The Hall of State was constructed in 1936 to serve as a shrine to Texas history and host the Texas Centennial Exposition and the Greater Texas and Pan-American Exposition in 1937. In 1938, the Dallas Historical Society took over management of the Hall. It now serves as home to the Society, shares free exhibits of Texas history, and rooms can be rented for events.

When visitors first approach the Hall of State, the vast greatness is overpowering. The gold-leafed bronze statue, *The Tejas Warrior* by Allie Victoria Tennant hovers over the entrance, welcoming visitors into the celebration of greatness. Once inside, the Hall of Heroes spotlights men important to the formation of Texas: Stephen F. Austin, Sam Houston, Mirabeau Lamar, Thomas Rusk, William B. Travis, James Fannin—captured in bronze statue by Pompeo Coppini. Past the Hall of Heroes, the Gold Medallion is the focal point of The Great Hall. A five point star, encompassed by female symbols of the six flags of Texas, hangs twelve feet in diameter, and is skirted on either side by 30-foot high murals depicting Texas' history. Extraordinary chandeliers hang from the stenciled ceiling. Fossilized shellstone columns add regalness to the mosaic flooring.

On either side of the Hall of Heroes are two rooms—four total—named for the cardinal directions. Each room speaks the flavor of the area of Texas it represents. East Texas shares the oil boom, west shows the pioneer and cowboy spirit with an emphasis on ranching. Old Man Texas holds dear Dallas and Fort Worth in the North room while South Texas' Mexican influence shines through the goddess mural.

As a whole, the Hall of State is an extraordinary example of Art Deco architecture. The Dallas Historical Society has rotating exhibits throughout the year and provides outreach and teacher programs aligned with state educational objectives. Online, the DHS also provides many downloadable resources, including the Hall of State Tour, information about Sam Houston, Dallas area History, and various student activity pages and programs (www.dallashistory.org). Exhibits are open Monday through Saturday 9:00 a.m. to 5:00 p.m., and Sunday 1:00 p.m. until 5:00 p.m.

TEXAS FUN FACT:

Pompeo Coppini, born in Italy, has 36 monuments, 16 portrait statues, and 75 portrait busts on display in the United States. His work includes the *Terry's Texas Rangers* monument on the Capitol grounds and *Alamo Cenotaph* in San Antonio.

Luckenbach

412 Luckenbach Town Loop

Fredericksburg, TX 78624

(830) 997-3224

www.luckenbachtexas.com

For those ready for a walk on the wilder side, Luckenbach is the place. The town's philosophy of "Everybody's Somebody in Luckenbach" was established way back in its humble beginnings as a trading post in 1849, as business was held with pioneer farmers and Comanche Indians alike.

The town was sold in 1970 to Hondo Crouch, who immediately declared himself mayor and continued the tradition of bringing folks together, but this time with good times and great music. After his death in 1976, the folks around town continue the traditions he set in place, such as the Ladies State Chili Bust and the Mud Dauber Festival, or just sitting together, playing dominoes and whistling along with the music on stage.

1997 brought fame to the little town, forever immortalized with Willie Nelson and Waylon Jennings' recording of "Luckenbach, Texas (Back to the Basics)", written by Bobby Emmons and Chips Moman. Fame, however, has not changed the area. Free music is scheduled every day of the week, with an occasional ticketed event (only if the entertainment charges for the show). Folks gather in and around the bar and general store, under the oaks, enjoying the kindred spirits that bring them together.

The town is open for visitors 10:00 a.m. until 9:00 p.m. daily…sometimes later.

Odessa Meteor Crater

3100 Meteor Crater Road

Odessa, TX 79763

(432) 385-0850 or 381-0946

www.odessahistory.com/crater.htm

The Odessa Meteor Crater is the second largest meteor crater in the United States at 550 feet in diameter and an original depth of 100 feet. It was originally found in 1892 by a local farmer searching for a lost calf; however, without the tools and knowledge base to identify the meteorites, it was thought of as a blow out hole, known by locals but not seen as important. In the 1920s, the Barringer family researched the area, identifying the area as a meteor crater. The Barringers tried to purchase the land from Texas and Pacific Land and Trust, but the land is oil-rich, and the Trust did not release it.

In 1926, Dr. E.H. Sellards found the crater while working as a researching geologist for the University of Texas and wrote a number of papers on the subject. Little was done about this re-discovery until 1935, when Dr. Harvey Nininger and his son Bob brought a magnetic balance (precursor to the metal detector) to the site and recovered 34 pounds of meteorites within the first two days. Dr. Lincoln LaPaz, another meteorite-phile convinced Ector County to let him excavate in search of a large meteorite by promising tourist interest and therefore increased revenue for the county. He began in 1939, but after hitting a large limestone plate, he and Dr. Sellards abandoned the project. We now know that the six tons of small meteorites recovered were the results of the large explosion caused by the meteor's impact on earth.

Interest in the crater has faded in and out through the years—research as well as public interest. The Odessa Meteor Crater was designated as a national landmark in 1965, but many did not see the importance, and the site was used as a dump and popular drinking/graffiti area. The wooden stairs in the shaft Sellards and LaPaz used in search of the large meteor were set on fire. (The shaft is now sealed with cement). Disinterest in its preservation moved the site to the "endangered historical site" list, and in the late 1990's, the county and state have paved the road to the park, put up picnic areas, and built a new museum with caretaker living quarters. Informational signs share the story of the crater with science-minded visitors as a newfound interest in the significance of the site is developed. Although the Thomas Rodman Museum is only open on weekends— Saturday 10:00 a.m. to 5:00 p.m., and Sunday 1:00 p.m. until 5:00 p.m.— self guided touring is offered daily from 9:00 a.m. until 6:00 p.m. The informational signs provide ample information to guide tourists, but if a meteorite view is desired, schedule visits when the museum is open.

TEXAS FUN FACT:

The "official flying mammal" of Texas is the Mexican free-tailed bat.

Palo Alto Battlefield National Historic Site

1623 Central Blvd

Brownsville, TX 78520-8326

(956) 541-2785

www.nps.gov/paal

After the United States annexed Texas, Mexico declared war on April 23, 1846 in retaliation. Mexican General Mariano Arista advanced troops north to Brownsville while United States General Zachary Taylor led troops south from Corpus Christi to meet in defense. Cannons rumbled between the armies, and after four hours of fighting, General Arista withdrew the troops for lack of ammunition. General Taylor called a cease fire as well, and the U.S. troops set up camp. The next morning, the Mexican army left early for Resaca de la Palma, where the U.S. troops followed to defeat Mexico. President James K. Polk declared war on May 13, and the war lasted two years. It came to an end in February, 1848, with the signing of the Treaty of Guadalupe Hidalgo, granting the United States California, Arizona, New Mexico, Rio Grande area of Texas, and parts of Utah, Nevada, and Colorado.

Today, Palo Alto's 3,400 acre National Historic Site is much like that of 1846. Native vegetation still populated the southern tip of Texas. An information-lined trail leads to the battlefield area. The historical significance of the war, as well as an abundance of wildlife in the area draws visitors to the site. Although young, the park is dedicated to sharing the stories that the two nations share. The park is approximately five miles north of Brownsville at the intersection of FM 1847 and FM 511. The Visitor Center is on 1847, north of the intersection. Tourists can view a 15-minute video about the battle and see exhibits signifying importance and effects of the Mexican War.

The park and visitor center is open 8:00 a.m. to 4:30 p.m. daily and is closed New Year's Day, Thanksgiving, and Christmas. The Palo Alto Battlefield National Historic Site offers a Junior Ranger Program. Booklets can also be downloaded from the website and mailed to Brownsville.

Rangerette Showcase

1100 Broadway

Kilgore, TX 75662-3299

(903) 983-8265

www.rangerette.com

It's hard to envision high school and college football games without drill team performances, and the Kilgore Rangerettes are to thank. The Rangerettes came about in 1939 as part of a two-fold plan by Dean Dr. B. E. Masters to attract more female students and keep students in the stands during football halftime breaks (rather than under the bleachers partaking in improper activities). Dr. Masters hired Miss Gussie Nell Davis for the challenge, and in September 1940, the Rangerettes debuted as the first dancing drill team in the nation. Their legacy lives on in schools throughout the United States, as nearly every high school and college now has a dancing drill team as part of their extracurricular programs.

The Rangerettes are still in action as well. Donned in the traditional red blouse, blue skirts, and white arm gauntlets, belt, hat and boots, the team is best known for their outstanding high kicks and show-stopping choreography. They are invited to perform at sporting events and celebrations all over the world, including the New Year's Cotton Bowl Classic in Dallas every year since 1951.

The Rangerette Showcase is in the Physical Education Complex at Kilgore College, and contains Miss Gussie Nell Davis' photograph collection. Together with other photos, former Rangerettes created the Rangerette Scrapbook, paying tribute to each year's accomplishments and highlights. Other items belonging to Miss Davis are also available to view, as well as costumes and props used by the Rangerettes throughout the years. A sixty-person theater "showcases" films and slideshows about the team's legacy while two mounted televisions show clips of performances. The Showcase is open Monday through Friday, 10:00 a.m. to 4:00 p.m., and Saturdays 10:00 a.m. to 4:00 p.m.

Washington-on-the-Brazos State Historical Site

P.O. Box 305

Washington, TX 77880-0305

(936) 878-2214

www.tpwd.state.tx.us/spdest/findadest/parks/washington_on_the_brazos/

Washington was established in 1821 on the banks of the Brazos, as a Robinson settlement (one of Stephen F. Austin's "Old 300") that came to be known as "La Bahia". By 1835, Robinson's land was sold and the town was reestablished as Washington, named after one of the owners' hometown in Georgia. Because of its accessibility to the river, Sam Houston found it advantageous to house his military headquarters in Washington in preparation for revolt against Santa Anna's Mexico.

In March of 1836, Washington became known as "The Birthplace of Texas", when 59 elected municipal delegates gathered in General Sam Houston's military town to sign the Texas Declaration of Independence (signed March 2). The delegates, although afraid they were next in line for Santa Anna's raid, remained in Washington for 17 days to continue their responsibility. They wrote the Constitution of the Republic of Texas and established the ad interim government before joining the evacuating town in the "Runaway Scrape" to the Colorado River area.

After the victory of San Jacinto on April 21st, surviving residents of Washington returned, along with a slew of new settlers. In 1842, President Sam Houston moved the Capitol of the Republic from Austin to Washington, and the town boomed with business as the political center. Texas' plans for statehood brought the Capitol back to Austin in 1845, and town leaders' rejection of the railroad in the 1850's dwindled Washington down from the former buzzing trade center. Anson Jones, Texas' last president, retired to nearby Barrington.

The Washington-on-the-Brazos State Historical Site encompasses a number of attractions on its 293 acres. Ticketed attractions include a guided tour of Independence Hall and the Washington Townsite, the Star of the Republic Museum, and the Barrington Living History Farm. Although much of the Washington-on-the-Brazos State Historical Site is ticketed, WOTB is one of the few state historical sites that does not charge an entrance fee. It is quite possible to spend a significant amount of time walking the area on the self-guided tour or picnicking by the Brazos. For history buffs, is well worth the time to visit the Birthplace of Texas. The walking trails have informational markers, explaining the history of the area. The Visitor Center provides information about the past as well, although it is primarily focused on the history of the paid attraction sites in the park. The park is open daily from 8:00 a.m. until sundown, and the Visitor Center is open daily 9:00 a.m. to 5:00 p.m. Group meeting facilities are also available; see the website for reservation details.

TEXAS FUN FACT:

Washington did not assume its current name of Washington-on-the-Brazos until after the Civil War.

XIT Museum
108 East 5th Street
Dalhart, TX 79022
(806) 244-5390
www.xitmuseum.com

In 1879, the State of Texas set aside three million acres of land in the Panhandle area as funding for the new State Capitol Building. What became known as the "Capitol Syndicate"—a group of investors from Chicago—agreed to complete the $3 million Capitol Building in exchange for the three million acres of land. First intentions were to sell the land, but upon investigation, the Syndicate decided that it was more profitable to run the land as a ranch until land prices went up. So, the XIT Ranch was born.

The Syndicate still needed money, however, to start the ranch and complete the Capitol construction. John Farwell, one of the Syndicate members, went to Great Britain and sold $10 million worth of bonds for the newly created "Capitol Freehold Land and Investment Company of London". The money allowed the completion of both projects under the Capitol Syndicate's responsibility; they finished the Capitol Building, fenced in the XIT (1,500 miles), and raised longhorn cattle (an average of 150,000 head after 1887).

When the London bonds matured, the XIT did not show itself as profitable as hoped. The Syndicate started selling cattle and pieces of the XIT in order to pay off investors. The ranch operated until 1912, and the last bit owned by descendants of the Syndicate was sold in 1963. Although the ranch is no more, the legends and stories associated with the largest fenced ranch live on today.

The XIT Museum contains exhibits about the ranch and area history as well as tools of the ranching trade. Displays of area wildlife, railroad history, and period clothing and furnishings help visitors picture life during the time of the XIT Ranch. A variety of changing exhibits show collections of typical "cowboy" items: hats, guns, saddles, brands, plus a few not-so-typicals as well. The museum also hosts youth programs and provides free "Educational Outreach Trunks" to area teachers, with information and activities about cowboys, early settlers, and Native Americans. Consult the website or call for information about the programs and Outreach Trunks.

The XIT Museum is open 9:00 a.m. to 5:00 p.m., Tuesday through Saturday. Donations are appreciated, but not required.

APPENDIX

AREA INDEX

Big Bend Country

- Amistad National Monument- Del Rio
- Border Patrol Museum- El Paso
- Chamizal National Museum- El Paso
- Chihuahuan Desert Gardens at the University of Texas El Paso- El Paso
- Ellen Noel Art Museum of the Permian Basin- Odessa
- El Paso Museum of Art- El Paso
- Fort Bliss Museums- El Paso
- George Paul Museum- Del Rio
- Haley Memorial Library and History Center- Midland
- Judge Roy Bean Center- Langtry
- Odessa Meteor Crater- Odessa
- Rio Bosque Wetlands Park- El Paso
- Val Verde Winery- Del Rio
- White-Pool House- Odessa

Gulf Coast

- 1861 Custom Home- Galveston
- Art Center of Corpus Christi- Corpus Christi
- Babe Didrikson Zaharias Museum- Beaumont
- Buu Mon Buddhist Temple- Port Arthur
- Cole Park- Corpus Christi
- Edison Plaza Museum- Beaumont
- Fire Museum of Texas- Beaumont
- Houston Arboretum and Nature Center- Houston
- Lillie and Hugh Roy Cullen Sculpture Garden- Houston
- Menil Collection- Houston
- Mercer Arboretum- Humble
- Mrs. Baird's Bakery- Houston
- Palo Alto Battlefield National Historic Site- Brownsville
- Piney Woods Country Wines- Orange

- Port of Houston Authority: Sam Houston Boat Tour- Houston
- Saint Paul's United Methodist Church- Houston
- Sea Center Texas- Lake Jackson
- Stark Museum of Art- Orange
- Texas Surf Museum- Corpus Christi
- Trinity Episcopal Church- Galveston
- Tyrrell Historical Library- Beaumont
- Wharton County Museum- Wharton

Hill Country

- Capitol Complex- Austin
- Cibolo Nature Center- Boerne
- Elisabet Ney Museum in Hyde Park- Austin
- First Presbyterian Church of Georgetown- Georgetown
- First State Bank of Uvalde- Uvalde
- Fort Martin Scott- Fredericksburg
- George Washington Carver Museum and Cultural Center- Austin
- John Nance Garner Museum: The Center for American History- Uvalde
- Llano County Museum- Llano
- Luckenbach- Fredericksburg
- Lyndon B. Johnson National Historic Park- Johnson City
- Lyndon B. Johnson State Park and Historic Site: Sauer-Beckmann Living History Farmstead- Stonewall
- O. Henry House and Museum- Austin
- Polly's Chapel- Bandera
- Saint Peter the Apostle Catholic Church- Boerne
- Saint Stanislaus Polish Catholic Church- Bandera
- Sister Creek Vineyards- Sisterdale
- Texas Hills Vineyards- Johnson City
- Texas Military Forces Museum- Camp Mabry- Austin
- The Candle Factory- Georgetown
- Wimberly Glass Works, Inc.- San Marcos

Panhandle Plains

- 5 D Custom Hats- Abilene
- Alibates National Monument: Flint Quarries- Fritch
- Amarillo Zoo in Thompson Park- Amarillo
- Breedlove Dehydrating Plant- Lubbock
- Cap*Rock Winery- Lubbock
- Carson County Square House Museum Complex- Panhandle
- Church of Heavenly Rest, Episcopal- Abilene
- Conrad Hilton- Hilton Museum in Cisco
- Deaf Smith County Museum- Hereford
- Hutchinson County Historical Museum
- James Leddy Boots- Abilene
- Lake Meredith National Recreation Area- Fritch
- Llano Estacado Winery- Lubbock
- Old Jail Art Museum- Albany
- Mrs. Baird's Bakery- Abilene
- Mrs. Baird's Bakery- Lubbock
- National Ranching Heritage Center- Lubbock
- Texas Panhandle War Memorial- Amarillo
- The Paramount- Abilene
- Wichita Falls Railroad Museum- Wichita Falls
- XIT Museum- Dalhart

Piney Woods

- Big Thicket National Preserve- Kountze
- Brookshire's World of Wildlife Museum and Country Store- Tyler
- Durst-Taylor Historical House and Gardens- Nacogdoches
- Lanana Creek Trail- Nacogdoches
- Light Crust Doughboys Museum- Quitman
- Marvin United Methodist- Tyler
- Old Nacogdoches University Building- Nacogdoches
- Rangerette Showcase- Kilgore
- Sam Houston Memorial Museum Complex- Huntsville

- Sam Houston Regional Library and Research Center: 1848 Gillard-Duncan House 1883 Norman House and Jean & Price Daniel House- Liberty
- Smith County Museum- Tyler
- Sterne-Hoya Home- Nacogdoches
- Texas Basket Company- Jacksonville
- Tyler Municipal Rose Garden- Tyler

Prairies and Lakes

- Amon Carter Museum- Fort Worth
- Bell County Museum- Belton
- Bureau of Engraving and Printing- Fort Worth
- Cameron Park- Waco
- Central Christian Church- Greenville
- Central Presbyterian Church- Paris
- Central Texas Area Museum- Salado
- Central Texas Oil Patch Museum- Luling
- Fort Hood- Killeen
- Gonzales Historical Tours- Gonzales
- Gonzales Memorial Museum - Gonzales
- Hall of State- Dallas
- Independence Tours- Independence
- Kimbell Art Museum- Fort Worth
- Mary Kay Ash: Mary Kay Museum - Addison
- Mrs. Baird's Bakery- Fort Worth
- Nocona Athletic Goods Company- Nocona
- Old Jail Museum- Gonzales
- Saint Francis Church on the Brazos- Waco
- Saints Cyril and Methodius Catholic Church- Shiner
- Sid Richardson Museum- Fort Worth
- Spoetzl Brewery- Shiner
- Washington-on-the-Brazos State Historical Site- Washington

South Texas Plains

- Fort Sam Houston- San Antonio
- Goliad's Historic Downtown Square
- Guenther House- San Antonio
- Japanese "Sunken" Garden- San Antonio
- La Villita- San Antonio
- Mrs. Baird's Bakery- San Antonio
- San Antonio Missions National Park- San Antonio
- Shrine of La Virgen de San Juan del Valle- San Juan
- The Alamo- San Antonio

Acknowledgements

"Countless people have made this book possible."

It seems like every book I open, I read these words, but after completing my first "name on the cover" book, I realize how true this is. My family traveled all around our great state in the creation of FREE TEXAS, and encountered numerous folks—from Mary Ann McNamara, volunteer county museum docent, to Dee, the breakfast hostess—National Park Rangers Dean Watkins in the panhandle to Buzz Botts on the coast—and everyone in between; each person we experienced went into the creation of this book. Stories were abound, from loyal family and friends who "always knew you'd be a writer, Tab" to supportive strangers, interested in Mr. Bilodeau's book concept. With much appreciation, I thank you.

While researching the attractions—finding stories—most of the information found was through a combination of visiting, talking with, or site-specific website research of each attraction. Resource information is listed before each entry, as the stories and experience I share are because of the attractions themselves. When I needed more information—whether it was clarification or additional details, I found the Handbook of Texas online website especially helpful: www.tsha.utexas.edu/handbook/online. There's a wealth of knowledge from various resources, gathered together from around the Lone Star State by the University of Texas in Austin. Many thanks to ya'll, too. Hook 'em Horns!

There are many more stories to share about Texas—it was exceedingly difficult to narrow free Texas attractions down to a manageable list. I know there are more out there—more stories, more attractions, more everything—we are a great and large state, with much to share. For your personal old favorites or new discoveries, please write them in your copy, or writer's notebook, or laptop journal. Because we remember and tell others, the stories of our past continue to live on.

About the author

Tab Lloyd was born Tammi Ann Braswell in Houston, 1969. There was something about that year that made her birth name, and all its variations, a popular choice for the time. Could it have been the popularity of the previous decade's "Tammy and the Bachelor" when the 1959 teenagers finally grew up and had kids? Some things can never be known, but by the age of ten, she was tired of being one of many, and had grown weary of singing shoe salesmen ("Tammy, Tammy, Tammy is in love!") That year, she changed her Tammi to the unusual acronym, "T.A.B."

By her junior year in high school, she had met her match—Stuart Lloyd. Not only is their relationship unforgettable, but when they married in 1991, her name became unforgettable. Now known as Tab Lloyd, she had the perfect name for a writer.

Writing has always been a part of Tab. She's enjoyed storytelling since her beginnings. These days, she shares her passion for stories (appreciation and creation) with her husband—Stu, two sons—Mike and Connor, and the third grade students in her Central Texas classroom.

About the artist

Stuart Lloyd enjoys photography and computer graphics as a hobby, and doesn't think he deserves credit for his photo contributions in this book.

But he does.

PHOTOS

Churches: Saint Paul's United Methodist Church in Houston
Famous People: Sam Houston Statue in Huntsville
Trade: 5D Custom Hats & Leather in Abilene
Art: The Art Center of Corpus Christi
Beer and Wine: Spoetzl Brewery in Shiner
Farms and Gardens: Sauer-Beckmann Living History Farmstead in Stonewall
Outside: Cole Park in Corpus Christi
Military: Stuart tank at 4th Infantry Division Museum on Fort Hood
Historical Places: Historical Homes in Independence
History Museums: Llano County Museum in Llano
Uniquely Texas: Post Office in Luckenbach

Printed in the United States
203619BV00001B/219/P